Imagining the Cognitive Science of Religion

SCIENTIFIC STUDIES OF RELIGION: INQUIRY AND EXPLANATION

Series editors: Luther H. Martin, Donald Wiebe, Radek Kundt, and Dimitris Xygalatas

Scientific Studies of Religion: Inquiry and Explanation publishes cutting-edge research in the new and growing field of scientific studies in religion. Its aim is to publish empirical, experimental, historical, and ethnographic research on religious thought, behaviour, and institutional structures. The series works with a broad notion of scientific that includes innovative work on understanding religion(s), both past and present. With an emphasis on the cognitive science of religion, the series includes complementary approaches to the study of religion, such as psychology and computer modelling of religious data. Titles seek to provide explanatory accounts for the religious behaviors under review, both past and present.

The Attraction of Religion, edited by D. Jason Slone and James A. Van Slyke
The Cognitive Science of Religion, edited by D. Jason Slone and William W. McCorkle Jr.
The Construction of the Supernatural in Euro-American Cultures, Benson Saler
Connecting the Isiac Cults, Tomáš Glomb
Contemporary Evolutionary Theories of Culture and the Study of Religion, Radek Kundt
Death Anxiety and Religious Belief, Jonathan Jong and Jamin Halberstadt
Gnosticism and the History of Religions, David G. Robertson
The Impact of Ritual on Child Cognition, Veronika Rybanska
Language, Cognition, and Biblical Exegesis, edited by Ronit Nikolsky, Istvan Czachesz, Frederick S. Tappenden & Tamas Biro
The Learned Practice of Religion in the Modern University, Donald Wiebe
The Mind of Mithraists, Luther H. Martin
Naturalism and Protectionism in the Study of Religion, Juraj Franek
New Patterns for Comparative Religion, William E. Paden
Philosophical Foundations of the Cognitive Science of Religion, Robert N. McCauley with E. Thomas Lawson
Religion, Disease, and Immunology, Thomas B. Ellis
Religion Explained?, edited by Luther H. Martin and Donald Wiebe
Religion in Science Fiction, Steven Hrotic
Religious Evolution and the Axial Age, Stephen K. Sanderson
The Roman Mithras Cult, Olympia Panagiotidou with Roger Beck
Solving the Evolutionary Puzzle of Human Cooperation, Glenn Barenthin
The Study of Greek and Roman Religions, Nickolas P. Roubekas
Understanding Religion Through Artificial Intelligence, Justin E. Lane

Imagining the Cognitive Science of Religion

Magic Bullets, Complex Theories,
Experimental Adventures

E. THOMAS LAWSON

BLOOMSBURY ACADEMIC
LONDON · NEW YORK · OXFORD · NEW DELHI · SYDNEY

BLOOMSBURY ACADEMIC
Bloomsbury Publishing Plc
50 Bedford Square, London, WC1B 3DP, UK
1385 Broadway, New York, NY 10018, USA
29 Earlsfort Terrace, Dublin 2, Ireland

BLOOMSBURY, BLOOMSBURY ACADEMIC and the Diana logo are trademarks of
Bloomsbury Publishing Plc

First published in Great Britain 2023

Copyright © E. Thomas Lawson, 2023

E. Thomas Lawson has asserted his right under the Copyright, Designs and
Patents Act, 1988, to be identified as Author of this work.

For legal purposes the Acknowledgments on p. x constitute an extension
of this copyright page.

All rights reserved. No part of this publication may be reproduced or transmitted
in any form or by any means, electronic or mechanical, including photocopying,
recording, or any information storage or retrieval system, without prior
permission in writing from the publishers.

Bloomsbury Publishing Plc does not have any control over, or responsibility for, any third-
party websites referred to or in this book. All internet addresses given in this book were
correct at the time of going to press. The author and publisher regret any inconvenience
caused if addresses have changed or sites have ceased to exist, but can accept no
responsibility for any such changes.

A catalogue record for this book is available from the British Library.

A catalogue record for this book is available from the Library of Congress.

ISBN: HB: 978-1-3503-5586-6
PB: 978-1-3503-5587-3
ePDF: 978-1-3503-5588-0
eBook: 978-1-3503-5589-7

Series: Scientific Studies of Religion: Inquiry and Explanation

Typeset by Deanta Global Publishing Services, Chennai, India

To find out more about our authors and books visit www.bloomsbury.com and
sign up for our newsletters

For
Ruth, Sonya, and Jennifer
and
Pascal, Bob, Joel, Brian, and Michal
and
Jason, Todd and Lee

Contents

Preface ix
Acknowledgments x

Introduction 1

1 Toward a Cognitive Science of Religion 11

PART I Theoretical Issues in the Cognitive Science of Religion 21

2 Magic Bullets and Complex Theories 23

3 The Wedding of Psychology, Ethnography, and History: Methodological Bigamy or Tripartite Free Love? 29

4 Cognitive Categories, Cultural Forms, and Ritual Structures 35

5 Evoked and Transmitted Culture 54

PART II Cognition and the Imagination 57

6 Cognitive Constraints on Imagining Other Worlds 59

7 The Explanation of Myth and Myth as Explanation 70

viii CONTENTS

8 Psychological Perspectives on Agency 87

9 How to Create a Religion 115

PART III Cognition, Culture, and History 123

10 History in Science 125

11 The Cognitive Science of Religion and the Growth of Knowledge 131

12 Counterintuitive Notions and the Problem of Transmission: The Relevance of Cognitive Science for the Study of History 143

PART IV Beyond Theory 159

13 Experimental Adventures 161

Conclusion 167

Index 169

Preface

This book is a collection of my single-authored essays, some new, some vintage. They disclose my understanding of the issues that characterize the cognitive science of religion (CSR), which now is more accurately called the cognitive and evolutionary science of religion (CESR). I have noticed, however, that many authors still prefer to employ the acronym CSR, perhaps for sentimental reasons. It is also the case, however, that it is possible and, in fact, quite useful to distinguish cognitive processes from their evolutionary roots and to engage in theoretical and experimental work that focuses on either scientific endeavor. One of the reasons for the impressive growth of CSR is that various scholars have recognized the useful division of labor and chosen to examine the processes that most concern them. For example, one can ask questions and propose hypotheses about the structure of a process, its origins, and its functions. Take, for example, the cognitive process of agency detection. A theorist may focus on the process of differentiating intentional and accidental motion, agency detection and theory of mind, hyperactive (hypersensitive) agency detection, by-product theorizing and adaptation theorizing, and so on. One thing is certain, and that is CSR, or CESR, if you prefer, is growing rapidly and that is good.

Acknowledgments

This book is dedicated to my wife and two daughters and five of my closest friends. All of them have made my life and my intellectual endeavors a joy to pursue because they were always ready to give advice and tell me when I was wrong. I also wish to thank Lily McMahon and Akshaya Ravi Pemmasani for all of there hard work as the editors of this book.

I wish to thank the journals and publishing houses that have not only published my work but given permission to reprint them: Bloomsbury Press, Brill Academic Publishers, Oxford University Press, Cambridge University Press, Open Court/ Cricket, Rowman and Littlefield Publishing Group, Berghahn Books, and e-Rhizome. The following are the papers reproduced in the book:

1. "Towards a Cognitive Science of Religion," in *Numen*, Brill Academic Publishers, September 2000

2. "Myth as Explanation and the Explanation of Myth," *Journal of the American Academy of Religion* XLVI/4, December 1978, Oxford University Press

3. "The Wedding of Psychology, Ethnography and History: Methodological Bigamy or Tripartite Free Love?" in *Theorizing Religions Past*, edited by H. Whitehouse and L. H. Martin, Altamira Press, Rowman and Littlefield Publishing Group, 2004

4. "Psychological Perspectives on Agency," in *Religion in Mind*, edited by Jensine Andresen, Cambridge: Cambridge University Press, 2001

5. "Cognitive Constraints on Imagining Other Worlds," in *Sci_Fi in the Mind's Eye Open Court/Cricket*, edited by Margret Grebowicz, 2007

6. "Cognitive Categories, Cultural Forms, and Ritual Structures," in *Cognitive Aspects of Religious Symbolism*, edited by P. Boyer, Cambridge University Press, 1992

7. "How to Create a Religion, eRhizome e-Rhizome," 1 (2), 2019, 132–7, ISSN 2571-242X https://doi.org/10.5507/rh.2019.007

8. "Counterintuitive Notions and the Problem of Transmission: The Relevance of Cognitive Science for the Study of History," published by Berghahn Books, New York

9. "History in Science" in *Evolution, Cognition and the History of Religions: Festschrift in Honor Armin W. Geertz,* Edited by Anders Klostergaard Petersen, Ingvild Saelid Gillus, Luthier H. Martin, Jeppe Sinding Jensen and Jesper Sorensen, Brill Academic Publishers, 2019

10. "The Cognitive Science of Religion and the Growth of Knowledge in Religion Explained?" Edited by Luther H Martin and Donald Wiebe, Bloomsbury Press, 2017

Introduction

The purpose of this Introduction is twofold: to tell you what is in this book and also how I became interested in a scientific study of religion, an interest which led to becoming deeply involved in establishing a new discipline, the cognitive science of religion.

In February 1961, I joined the newly established Department of Philosophy and Religion at Western Michigan University in Kalamazoo, Michigan, had completed my field examinations at the University of Chicago, had defended my special statement before the faculty, but was still writing my doctoral dissertation. I knew I was going to be very busy engaged in teaching and writing at the same time. I had spent a great deal of intellectual energy studying both philosophy and religion at Chicago but felt woefully unprepared for the role of the teacher of philosophy and religion in a public university. I had studied and taken examinations in the history of religions, religion and art, religion and the personality sciences, the history of Christian thought, Old and New Testament, philosophy of religion, ethics, and a year-long course on Plato and Aristotle, and was writing my dissertation on comparing the philosophical theology of Paul Tillich and Charles Hartshorne.

I decided that, while I was scheduled to teach courses in the introduction to the religions of the world as well as a general studies course in arts and ideas, I would introduce myself to faculty members in other departments and find out how they went about doing their jobs. I was fortunate to meet faculty in psychology (Jack Michaels and Dick Malott), anthropology (Al Jacobs), economics (Louis Junker), linguistics (Bob Palmatier), and political science (Sam Clark, Roy Olton, Claude Phillips, and Milton Greenberg). All of these scholars seemed to have reasonably clear subject matters and methods for dealing with them. I did not. (Later, I also became friends with faculty in computer science and English Language and Literature.)

At the University of Chicago, I had developed an interest in the natural and social sciences largely by sitting in science and philosophy courses, reading philosophers' books such as Alfred North Whitehead's *Science and the Modern World* and *Adventures and Ideas,* struggling through *Process and Reality,* and entertaining the idea that a scientific study of religious thought and behavior might be possible. My closest friend Hans Penner and I had many discussions about a scientific study of religion and he even published an article entitled: "Is a Science of Religion Possible?" Some of the faculty at the University of Chicago had argued that outside of the social sciences, a *religionswissenschaft* was not only possible but could be found in the works of scholars such as Mircea Eliade, Joachim Wach, and Joseph Kitagawa, but I found this concept difficult to understand and, in fact, incoherent. It seemed to be neither science nor the humanities.

In my new job I embarked, therefore, on a journey to find out what science was and how, if at all, it could be applied to the study of religion. This involved a great deal of reading and many conversations. Particularly helpful were my conversations with the behavioral psychologists, the lone linguistic scholar in the English department Bob Palmatier, the economist Louis Junker, and the political scientists Claude Phillips, Milton Greenberg, Sam Clark, and Rex Olton. My questions to them were always: What do you do? How do you do it? How do you know you are successful? At the same time, I kept asking myself: What do I need to know to do something like these scholars were doing with the subject matter with which I was dealing? My subject matter seemed to be rather messy and the methods in hiding.

While I was having fun exploring the world of science, the world was going on with its business and some of it was not good. Martin Luther King was assassinated in April 1968, and because of my involvement in the civil rights movement in Chicago, in raising money for Nelson Mandel's defense at his treason trial, I had been asked by the Black students at our university to become the adviser to the Black Action Movement (BAM). One day in a conversation with Frank Jackson, a leader of BAM, he suggested that I read Noam Chomsky. I take students seriously and so, a few weeks later, as I was browsing through a pile of used books, I came across a book, *Syntactic Structures*, by Noam Chomsky and, remembering Jackson's recommendation, bought it.

What a revelation! Here was a book which seemed to show that despite the differences, sometimes radically so, among the many languages of the world, all languages appeared to be governed by certain fundamental principles. I was elated because I thought that if this was true of language, a clearly cultural phenomenon, why could it not be true of cultural systems such as religion? Cross-culturally both religion and language certainly varied, but perhaps there were underlying principles which constrained their form.

The next time I saw Frank, I told him how excited I was to read Chomsky and how important it was to the problem I was attempting to solve. He wanted to know which book I had read. When I told him I had read *Syntactic Structures* he said, "Oh No! I intended for you to read his *political* writings!" Happy mistake! This occurred in late 1968. In the next few years, I began a concentrated study of linguistics starting with *"Aspects of a Theory of Syntax"* but with no idea of how the methods that linguists employed could be applied to the subject matter of religion, but I was convinced that linguistics was in

INTRODUCTION

some way a key to explaining religious thought and behavior—and said so to my students. At the same time, I was still enamored by the writings of Claude Levi-Strauss, particularly his claims that peoples' construction of myth revealed quite specific ways in which the human mind worked, specifically by binary operations. My essay in this volume on "Myths as Explanation and the Explanation of Myth" (Chapter 7) reveals some of those interests in Levi Straussian structuralism. Levi-Strauss provided me with my initial introduction to issues about how the human mind works and was, therefore, my first introduction to cognitive science. Levi-Strauss had become interested in Roman Jakobson's work on phonology, a branch of linguistics, and particularly his explorations of distinctive features.

In 1975, I attended a conference sponsored by the International Association for the History of Religions in Lancaster, England, where I met Donald Wiebe and renewed my acquaintance with my great friend Luther Martin. Both of them, like me, were in search of a scientific study of religion. It was in Lancaster where I made my first attempt to apply what I thought was a linguistic method inspired by both Chomsky and Levi-Strauss in a paper entitled "Ritual as Language." The paper was, in fact, more Levi Straussian structuralism than Chomskyian and, frankly, I thought, was a complete failure, although the audience did not and by their response seemed to find it very interesting. Michael Pye, an editor of *Religion*, was in the audience and liked it so much that he recommended its publication in that journal, so perhaps it had some redeeming qualities.

In 1977, I was fortunate enough to be named a Fellow of the *Council for Philosophical Studies* and was chosen to attend an eight-week summer workshop on *Biology, Philosophy and the Social Sciences* at The Colorado College in Colorado Springs. Some of my teachers were Stephen Gould, Richard Levins, Margery Grene, Alan Donagan, Anthony Kenny, and William Wimsatt. In Chapter 13, "Experimental Adventures," I discuss the importance of my study of Harvester Ants in the Garden of the Gods with Richard Levins so I will only allude to it here.

Between 1977 and 1985, I slowly launched my study of linguistics, continuing to be convinced that the methods it employed had application to religious thought and behavior in class and in conversations with my students and most of all with Robert McCauley, my student in the early 1970s and friend and colleague, while he was a graduate student first in religion and then in philosophy of science at the University of Chicago. That friendship proved to be a creative relationship and has continued until this day!

In August of 1985, I read a paper on the application of linguistic theory to religious phenomena at the meeting of the *International Association of the History of Religions* in Sydney, Australia, to stunned silence. There were no questions after I had completed my presentation so I got out of there as soon as possible and went to lunch. At the table, the person next to me asked me why I looked so glum, I responded that I was depressed by the zero response to my paper. When I explained that I was attempting the application of linguistic method to religious thought and behavior, he excitedly told me that he was working on the same thing! His name was Frits Staal. He gave me the reference to a paper that he had written. I read it as soon as I returned from Australia and thought that his approach, while interesting, missed the real possibilities provided by the linguistic method. (McCauley and I discuss his work in *Rethinking Religion: Connecting Cognition and Culture.*) We could see that he was onto something but not getting the most interesting story, the most interesting possibilities that the methods of linguistics provided, especially the *internal structure* of a linguistic act.

When I returned to the United States, I immediately got in touch with McCauley and told him that we had better get to work otherwise we would be scooped by Staal.

All of this takes some explaining. Between 1977 and 1985, I had begun to play with tree diagrams (which I had learned from the study of linguistics), trying to illustrate how ritual actions had a structure similar to that of sentences, the basic unit of language. I conjectured that such actions being cognitive products could also be formally represented in ways similar to sentences. If that was the case, that meant that cognitive science was capable of providing the set of ideas and methods which could make sense of religious ritual acts. None of this was very clear in my head, but I did not want to give up the idea. I kept trying, therefore, to write about this idea. At some point in the mid-1970s, I had written enough for it to at least appear to be interesting. Taking my intellectual life in my hands, I called up Bob McCauley and asked him if I could come down to Indiana to show him what I had come up with. I was especially impressed with the knowledge he had gained in the philosophy of science at Chicago and knew that he would be a good critic. I traveled down to Indiana and showed him the paper with its diagrams I had constructed and asked him whether the ideas and their formal representation were trivial or not. After going through the paper, his immediate judgment was that the ideas were trivial. Deflated, I asked him if he had any scotch? He did, and we had a drink or two. Then he said: "Show me that paper again." After going through the paper, a second time he said: "You know, I don't think this is trivial." Elated, I suggested that we scrap what I had done and work on a new paper together that developed the ideas I had conjectured. After that we exchanged papers back and forth working out the details. The result became an early version of Chapter 5 in *Rethinking Religion.* Ideas that went into that early work were the content of my presentation in Australia!

So, between 1977 and 1985, Bob and I had been working on the ideas that would become chapter 5 of *Rethinking Religion.* At some point, I started

INTRODUCTION

submitting a version of proto-chapter 5 for publication, first to the *Journal of the American Academy of Religion*, where one reviewer recommended publication and the other did not, ensuing in its rejection. Then the journal *Religion* with the same result and then *Current Anthropology*, which also rejected it despite a number of very positive reviews, one of which said something like: if this paper is published it will change the direction of anthropology!

When I returned from Australia in 1985 and after having discovered that Staal had similar ideas it made sense to recommend to McCauley that we write a book that presented a systematic treatment of how cognition and culture were connected with religious rituals as the subject matter and by employing some of the methods of linguistics. Little did we know that the publication of *Rethinking Religion*: *Connecting Cognition and Culture* would signal the start of a revolution in the study of religious thought and behavior and make a contribution to its development and spread. In fact, it succeeded in capturing the attention of scholars and students in both the humanities and the social sciences eager for a scientific study of religion. The book received many positive reviews in academic journals, especially in psychology, anthropology, and religious studies.

The first essay in this set of journeys in cognitive science (Chapter 1, "Toward a Cognitive Science of Religion") explores the theoretical territory of a cognitive approach to religion This essay employs one of the very first uses of the term "the cognitive science of religion." It was published ten years after *Rethinking Religion* as an attempt to alert students of religion in the various disciplines interested in religion, especially in the humanities that something was afoot in science that deserved their attention. Many scholars in anthropology, psychology, the history of religions, and religious studies have told me that it gave them a clue about why it might be important to give cognitive science a chance. In the same year, and also employing the term "cognitive science of religion," Justin Barret published an essay in *Trends in Cognitive Science*, analyzing the basic ideas that had been developed through the very creative years in the 1990s. My essay was published in *Numen: International Review for the History of Religions*.

I have divided this collection of essays into three parts: (1) Theoretical Issues in the Cognitive Science of Religion, (2) Cognition, Religion, and the Imagination, (3) Cognition, Culture, and History, and (4) Experimental Adventures. Each of these topics is closely related. Any subject in a scientific investigation will inevitably involve a theory of some sort. In Popperian terms, theories are conjectures about what is the case and must be capable of refutation. A conjecture represents a claim, a hypothesis, that something is the case and calls for evidence to back up the claim empirically or experimentally. The reader will see that my essays are replete with conjectures and hopefully also see that at least sometimes they provide the evidence to substantiate the claims I make. Chapter 2 focuses on those theories that act as magic bullets, which attempt to explain religion by a single concept such as superstition, illusion, the need for comfort, fear of death, and so on. Such a concept is supposed to account for a vast subject matter, "religion." My view is that all of them miss the fact that "religion" is an umbrella term covering many different cognitive processes, each of which requires an explanation.

Chapter 3 celebrates the wedding of the disciplines of psychology, ethnography, and history, which in its complexity avoids magic bullets at the celebration of cross-disciplinary cooperation. Behind the scenes in this essay were scientists engaged in actual discussion from various disciplines, all helping to establish a newly emerging inquiry in the 1990s and at the turn of the millennium, the discipline that came to be known as the cognitive science of religion: Bob McCauley in philosophy of science, Pascal Boyer in cognitive and evolutionary anthropology, Justin Barrett in psychology, Harvey Whitehouse in ethnography, Brian Malley and Ilkka Pyysiainen and Veikko Antonnen in comparative religion, Luther Martin and Donald Wiebe in the history of religion, and me in the philosophy of religion but moving into cognitive science. Stewart Guthrie in anthropology soon joined us. The discussions were fruitful and intense. Our initial meetings were held at the annual meetings of the Society for the Scientific Study of Religion but from the beginning, various members met at various workshops and conferences held at Cambridge University, Western Michigan University, and the University of Michigan

Chapter 4, "Cognitive Categories, Cultural Forms, and Ritual Structures," dives into the messy pool involved in connecting cognitive facts to cultural facts by focusing on ritual action. This essay was published in a book edited by Pascal Boyer, *Cognitive Aspects of Religious Symbolism*, and was the product of conversations I had with Pascal when he invited me, shortly after *Rethinking Religion* was published, to lead a seminar on cognition, culture, and religion at Cambridge University.

Chapter 5 is new and was written for this volume. It introduces to its readers the concept of *evoked culture*, a very controversial concept initially proposed by John Tooby and Leda Cosmides. I expect criticism for keeping this concept alive, especially by scholars entranced by neural plasticity and the heavy weight of "Culture."

The essays in the section on Cognition and the Imagination (Chapters 6–9) attempt to cast light on the role that imagination plays in scientific work and represents an attempt to show that the humanities is not alien to science. Every scientific process in some way or the other calls upon the imagination to do its work in extending our cognitive horizons. Chapter 6 dives into the imaginary worlds of science fiction and shows how the same processes that are memorable and transmittable and that play *a* role in religion enjoy a similar

INTRODUCTION

role in the imaginary world of fiction. It was published in *Sci Fi in the Mind's Eye*, edited by Margret Graber, and examines the limits of the imagination. Especially important is the concept of least resistance. Chapter 7, "The Explanation of Myth and Myth as Explanation," referred to earlier, is an early essay when I was still looking at structuralism through the eyes of Claude Levi-Strauss. Not enough attention has been paid to myth in CSR.

Chapter 8, "Psychological Perspectives on Agency," is my attempt to imagine the application of the concept of agency developed in psychology to religion. It focuses on the very important and imaginative work of the psychologist Alan Leslie, who not only understood the concept of agency but was able to show empirically and experimentally how it worked. My job was to show how all of this applies to religion.

Chapter 9, "How to Create a Religion," has a history. It started out as a lecture with slides and was delivered at Cambridge University and was meant to answer a challenge. Can all of your theories actually have an application in the real world? That was in 2011. Then, in 2013, I was invited to become acting director of LEVYNA, Laboratory for the Scientific Study of Religion, Masaryk University, Czech Republic. One of my tasks was to teach a course on the cognitive science of religion to a group of undergraduates. I used a version of this illustrated lecture to tempt the students to take the subject seriously and have fun at the same time. Then, just a few years ago, I was invited to write an essay for a new journal, *e-Rhizome*, and I transformed this lecture into an article for that journal.

The essays in the part "Cognition, Culture, and History" recognize that every scientific discipline not only has a history but is historical; for example, Charles Darwin's theory of natural selection is a temporal theory. Evolution takes time and is a process in time. I will let the essays in that section make the best case that can be made for the historical character of most and perhaps all disciplines. "History in Science," Chapter 10, calls attention to the relevance of the concept of history for all disciplines. It is a way of showing the relevance of the humanities for the sciences. Chapter 11, "The Cognitive Science of History and the Growth of Knowledge," argues that the cognitive science of religion is a progressive rather than a degenerative research program.

Chapter 12, "Counterintuitive Notions and the Problem of Transmission: The Relevance of Cognitive Science for the Study of History," was published in the journal *Historical Reflections* and was an attempt to generate a conversation between historians and cognitive psychologists by showing how certain psychological facts should play a role in historical narratives. I regard this as a breakthrough article because I actually got historians to listen to what I in another developing discipline was saying.

The last part, "Experimental Adventures," presents a highly personal journey that reveals the very slow process involved in my acquiring some of the knowledge necessary to join the exciting world of theoretical and experimental science.

Perhaps this is the place in this book to summarize the origin and early development of the cognitive science of religion.

In 1975, I delivered a lecture in Lancaster, the UK, at the quinquennial meeting of the International Association of the History of religions entitled "Ritual as Language," which, as I mentioned earlier, was my first attempt to apply some of the methods of linguistics to religious materials especially religious rituals. It had a strong structuralist tone. In 1975, I published a review of Dan Sperber's book *Rethinking Symbolism*. This book had a profound effect on my thinking and showed me how the cognitive aspects of linguistic theory could be applied to anthropological material in general and religious materials in particular. I used this book every year from then on in my classes. Between 1975 and 1985, Bob McCauley and I had many conversations about applying the methods of the emerging cognitive sciences culminating first in a paper subject to repeated rejection by scholarly journals and finally in a book, *Rethinking Religion: Connecting Cognition and Culture*, in 1990. In 1985, I presented a paper on ritual structures at the IAHR conference in Sydney, Australia, and by good fortune met Frits Staal, a meeting which spurred me to write a book with Bob McCauley on ritual. Between 1985 and 1990 (when *Rethinking Religion* was published by Cambridge University Press), I became the evangelist for a cognitive approach to religion, in my classes, at conferences, and when meeting new scholars. After the publication of that book, I was invited by Pascal Boyer to Cambridge University and we became very good friends. Then, in the early 1990s, I invited Dan Sperber and Pascal Boyer to give lectures at Western Michigan University and Pascal invited Bob McCauley and me to a workshop at Cambridge University, where we met Harvey Whitehouse. Then I held a conference at Western Michigan University with Bob McCauley, Harvey Whitehouse, Justin Barrett, and Brian Malley on issues in the cognitive science of religion. During the 1990s, I was invited to Denmark by Armin Geertz to discuss the application of cognitive science to religion as well as by Veikko Antonnen and Ilkka Pyysiainen in Helsinki Finland to do the same thing. It was at this meeting in Finland that I introduced Ilkka to the thought of Pascal Boyer, particularly Pascal's concept of the cognitive catalogue of the Supernatural, which, Ilkka told me, had a profound effect on his thinking. In 1993, Stewart Guthrie published *Faces in the Clouds* and became a member of the CSR movement. In the late 1990s and early 2000s, I had three brilliant students, Jason Slone, Todd Tremlin, and Joel Mort. I encouraged them to write their doctoral dissertations as books. Both Tremlin and Slone's books were published by Oxford University Press. Mort published parts of his dissertation as articles in various scholarly journals. Justin Barrett and I, in the late 1990s, had been working on designing experiments about

INTRODUCTION

ritual, and Justin, Pascal, and I were invited to make presentations at a workshop at the University of Michigan (where I met Ara Norenzayan and Scott Atran). Justin and I presented the results of our experimental work to an interested and appreciative audience. As the twentieth century was drawing to a close, all of us felt the need for a journal that would focus on issues in cognition and culture. During this time Harvey Whitehouse and Pascal Boyer were visiting me. Pascal, Justin, and I decided that we would establish such a journal. I had been the co-editor of the journal *Numen*, published by Brill Academic Publishers, and so had a good relationship with Hans van der Meij, an editor at Brill. I met Hans at Brill in Leiden and presented to the publishers the idea of such a journal. The response was not only positive but enthusiastic. I flew home happy and got to work: the first issue of the *Journal of Cognition and Culture* came out in 2000. The editors were Lawson, Boyer and Barrett.

In 2003, I attended the annual meeting of the Society for the Scientific Study of Religion in Norfolk, Virginia. Harvey Whitehouse and I were having a conversation when Harvey told me his ideas of an Institute of Cognition and Culture at Queen's University, Belfast, and invited me to come to Belfast to help him establish it. I asked my wife what she thought of the idea and whether she was willing to move to Belfast. She was enthusiastic about the idea, and so in June 2004, I retired from Western Michigan University and moved to Belfast in August 2004, where I became a member of the staff of the Institute of Cognition and Culture at Queen's University, Belfast, Northern Ireland. Joel Mort also moved to the ICC as a Distinguished International Fellow. The ICC enrolled its first students and it did not take long for students to graduate with their PhDs. CSR was on its way. Students were graduating and looking for jobs. Conferences were organized, and the IACSR was formed. The word was out to the larger academic community.

One conference was organized by Illa Pyysiainen and Veikko Antonnen and was held on the Island of Seili in Finland and was attended by Pascal Boyer, Bob McCauley, Harvey Whitehouse, Justin Barrett, Armin Geertz, Jesper Sorenson, Stewart Guthrie, Ilkka, Veikko, and me. It was at this conference that the concept of Hyperactive Agency Detection Device (HADD) was suggested by Bob McCauley and developed by Justin Barrett. Another meeting of most of these people was held at the Society for the Scientific Study of Religion Annual meeting in San Diego. We even met in 2000 at the annual meeting of the International Association of the History of Religions in Durban, South Africa. In these various meetings (Ann Arbor, Durban, Aarhus, Brno, San Diego, Seili, Helsinki, and Boston), an interdisciplinary conversation had begun that was developing a model for the cognitive science of *religion*. In fact, we began to see it as having all the properties of a standard model. Of course, as theoretical development proceeded apace, and experimentation developed the model itself has changed and became more sophisticated.

More and more, the group, which was first slowly and then rapidly increasing in size as scholars from various disciplines (anthropology, psychology, history, comparative religion, and evolutionary biology), began to identify themselves as cognitive scientists of religion.

Recently, I checked Google Scholar for citation classics (more than one thousand references) and found that Boyer's *Religion Explained*, Justin Barrett's *Exploring the Natural Foundations of Religion*, Lawson and McCauley's *Rethinking Religion*, McCauley and Lawson's *Bringing Ritual to Mind*, Harvey Whitehouse's *Modes of Religiosity*, and Stewart Guthrie's *Faces in the Clouds* had all achieved that status.

INTRODUCTION TO CHAPTER 1

"Towards a Cognitive Science of Religion" *was my farewell essay to the editorship of* Numen: International Review of the History of Religion, *a position I held with Hans Kippenberg for nearly twelve years (1988–2000). This essay was published in the same year that I assumed the editorship, with Pascal Boyer and Justin Barrett, of the* Journal of Cognition and Culture, *a position I still hold twenty-two years later. The essay places the cognitive science of religion squarely in the cognitive revolution and points to a remarkable cooperation between philosophers, cognitive and evolutionary psychologists, cognitive anthropologists, computer scientists, artificial intelligence, evolutionary biologists, and cognitive neuroscientists along with some brave souls in religious studies. Of particular importance is the fact that twenty-two years later the cognitive science of religion is thriving.*

1

Toward a Cognitive Science of Religion

It is difficult to miss the fact that the last fifty years has given birth to a revolution in the sciences. This revolution has transformed not only the way scientists theorize about the human mind but the means they have devised to test their theories. Cognitive science, which has emerged in the context of this revolution, has coordinated, distilled, and extended the particular explanatory theories of human cognition provided by cognitive psychology, cognitive anthropology, linguistics, artificial intelligence (AI), philosophy, neuroscience, and computer science. It has even begun to operate within the context of comparative religion. The purpose of this contribution is to discuss the relevance of cognitive science for the study of the religious ideas and practices of humankind by pursuing three questions: (1) Is a cognitive science of religion possible? (2) Is a cognitive science of religion necessary? (3) Is a cognitive science of religion emerging?

Is a Cognitive Science of Religion Possible?

Theorizing about religion as a *cultural* system is standard fare in the social sciences and has also had a great impact on studies in the humanities. Theorizing about religion as a set of cultural phenomena from a *cognitive* perspective is a more recent development. In fact, in many respects, a cognitive approach to cultural phenomena such as religion is quite novel, and because of such novelty, is capable of arousing intense suspicion and even antagonism. One of the main reasons for such a response to this new science has been the inevitable suspicion aroused whenever scholars make appeals to psychological explanations of sociocultural phenomena. The standard assumption in the social sciences and the humanities has been that only social and cultural methods can explain social and cultural facts. Of course, the possibility of a cognitive science of religion depends upon showing that cognitive explanations of sociocultural facts not only are possible but have already happened. If cognitive science has already been successful in developing interesting, powerful, and empirically tractable theories of one cultural form, then that success certainly would have relevance for a science of other cultural phenomena such as religion. And it is no longer much of a secret that a cognitive science of language, an eminently cultural phenomenon, is in full bloom and has been since the fifth decade of the twentieth century. Ever since the publication of Noam Chomsky's *Syntactic Structures* (1957), the cognitive study of language has made astonishing progress. Explanatory theories abound at the phonological, syntactic, and semantic levels of analysis. (For a recent popular account of the cognitive revolution in the study of language, see Steven Pinker's *The Language Instinct* [1994].)

In earlier theorizing about human languages, one feature of languages which had seemed to pose problems for cross-cultural generalizations had been their seemingly endless variability. Such variability seemed an obstacle to systematic study whether one focused upon the differences in sounds, the differences in word order, or the differences in meaning. The variety of languages and language forms in the world is immense not even taking local dialects into consideration. It would seem that no one scholar could ever hope to develop a significant command of all of these languages. So how could one produce a theory unless one had command of all of the facts? Scholars of religion who are equally cognizant of the great variety of religions and religious forms could take comfort in the massiveness of religious variety and settle for something less or something other than generalizations about religious phenomena. So, if, despite such variation, a cognitive science of language has in fact emerged, this gives scholars of religion hope that a similar cognitive science of religion could be developed.

Another feature of language worthy of note to scholars of religion is that, such diversity notwithstanding, the cognitive study of language has led to the development of theories about the underlying structure of language. Such a study has revealed that deep down languages are not that different from each other. In fact, not only have cognitive scientists developed powerful competence theories of the phonology, syntax, and semantics of human languages but they also have been successful in the discipline of pragmatics (see Sperber and Wilson, *Relevance*, 1986) where matters of performance take precedence over theories of linguistic competence. As the result of such studies in pragmatics, we now know much more about the structure of communication than we did before.

What the cognitive science of language has shown is that beneath the variability of language there is a commonality, or to be more precise, a set of principles which accounts for the complex character of linguistic phenomena. It is not variable all the way down. In fact, on the syntactic level of analysis, linguists have been able to demonstrate that there are certain universal constraints (known as Universal Grammar) on the formation of particular grammars. Beneath the surface complexity of human languages lies a set of principles which organize the sequences of words that make up sentences in quite specific ways. The result has been the development of interesting theories about the trajectory from sound to meaning.

The fact of the success of linguistics, therefore, is an existence proof of the possibility of a science of at least one form of culture, namely language. A cognitive science of religion would be possible if it could be shown that despite the obvious variability of religion across cultures and throughout history there lay a similar specifiable commonality. In the third section of this chapter, we shall address the evidence for such commonalities in the emerging cognitive science of religion.

Is a Cognitive Science of Religion Necessary?

Let us concede for the moment that a cognitive science of religion is possible. Such a concession does not, however, make it *necessary* for scholars of religion to actualize the possibility of a cognitive science of religion. Not every road that beckons needs to be trodden. In a world of many options perhaps there are better journeys to take. Why not, instead, continue to do what historians and anthropologists of religion have done so well? Our shelves are filled with careful historical studies of the development of particular religious traditions, fine-grained ethnographic studies of various societies, sophisticated philological studies essential for grasping the connotations and denotations of esoteric texts, powerful contextual studies of particular features of religious traditions, trenchant studies of the relationships between religious systems and political or economic systems, and even postmodernist critiques of the very possibility of objective scholarship of any kind in the human sciences. All these endeavors have contributed to a greater or lesser degree to our understanding of religious ideas, the practices they inform, the institutions they engender, and the controversies they generate. So why not stay the course and ignore the revolution?

Actually, no particular line of scientific inquiry *is* ever necessary. Refusing to engage in any kind of inquiry is always an option. And even science itself, as a highly specialized enterprise, does not require our commitment. Although human beings are gifted with inquisitive minds, it is quite possible to keep such inquisitiveness at bay and within bounds. Many individuals and groups of people have been and continue to be quite successful at restraining their inquisitiveness. And at times in human history inquiry into the nature of the physical world has been suppressed. At different times and places various social institutions have demonstrated at least an ambivalent attitude toward science, and on occasion, an active hostility toward it. Furthermore, it is only when such inquisitiveness is institutionalized and its development encouraged and supported with adequate resources that the sciences begin to bloom. Societies with only a rudimentary science have existed in the past and could exist again. There are no guarantees (see Robert McCauley, "Comparing the Cognitive Foundations of Religion and Science," 1998) that science will remain as a viable way of acquiring knowledge about ourselves and the world we occupy. Human beings are quite capable of settling for rumor, gossip, innuendo, unsubstantiated reports, and propaganda. Such predilections might even confer an evolutionary advantage!

But as part of the academy and wishing to see the discipline to which we have committed our lives make our knowledge of the world grow, there are good reasons for us to follow new paths of inquiry when they show promise of fulfilling our objectives. A sense of adventure might lead us into trouble, but sometimes the trouble is worth it if new discoveries beckon. So, despite such cautionary statements I wish to claim that a cognitive science of religion is necessary (in the sense of worthy of being done) because it will help lead us into deeper insights about symbolic-cultural systems such as religion. A cognitive science of religion certainly shows every promise of deepening our understanding of the cognitive constraints on cultural form. Those who are dedicated to cultural relativism and its cousin cultural determinism often give the impression that there are no limits on either the contents of our minds or the cultural products that issue forth from them. We have come to see through the insights of cognitive science that this is not the case. There *are* limits to cultural (and, a fortiori, religious) variability.

Of particular importance to the discipline of the history of religions at this time is the development of explanatory theories of religion by scholars who are not only tuned to the sciences but also have a deep knowledge of religious traditions. In our study of these religious traditions, our discipline has typically been long on interpretation and short on explanation. In other words, we have been focused more on problems of meaning and significance than problems of structure and cause. Making explanatory issues more central to our discipline (without denying the values of interpretation) promises to redress the imbalance between interpretive and explanatory concerns by deepening our understanding of the structure, acquisition, transmission, and communication of religious ideas and the practices they inform. So, a cognitive science of religion is necessary *if* we wish our knowledge of the systematicity of cultural forms to grow and especially if we desire more penetrating explanations of the structure and causes of religious ideas and practices.

Is a Cognitive Science of Religion Emerging?

As I have already argued, the best way to deal with the question of whether something is possible is to show that it has already been done. (In fact, the international journal *Trends in Cognitive Sciences* recently published an article by Justin Barrett, "Exploring the Natural Foundations of Religion," on the new cognitive science of religion [2000]). Some scholars who were interested in cultural phenomena such as religion and who had been paying close attention to the birth of the new science of the mind decided that it was worth employing the strategies of the cognitive sciences to religious materials. They decided to rethink *religionswissenschaft* by suggesting cognitive explanations of phenomena that had largely resided within the province of hermeneutics. So, for example, Dan Sperber reexamined issues concerning symbolism and meaning in *Rethinking Symbolism* (1975). In that by now classic work Sperber not only showed the weakness of semiotic approaches to the study of cultural forms but also showed that specific cultural activities such as the widespread use of symbolism are evidence of specific mental abilities each of which needs to be distinguished from each other and each of which has a causal role in cultural productions. In that book, he was able to at least highlight the differences between dictionary, encyclopedic, and symbolic knowledge and to demonstrate important properties of the latter. Sperber turned our attention to the variety of cognitive mechanisms we need to identify and describe if we are to have any hope of developing new and interesting theories about the cultural life of human beings.

One of the most interesting things about any scientific theory is that you never know whether what you are describing is going to be relevant to anything or not. A case in point is the many alternative geometries that mathematicians have constructed over the centuries which seemed to have no relevance to the world as we know it. And then in the twentieth century, it became apparent that such geometries were very useful indeed to modern physics. By adopting a cognitive perspective, Dan Sperber was able to make us rethink not only symbolism but the mind that produces it. (See Lawson, "Religious Ideas and Practices," 1999.) Rethinking symbolism led to the challenge to rethink religion, and more specifically to rethink how we go about studying religion from a cognitive scientific perspective. Suddenly a science that seemed only of marginal significance to cultural phenomena was seen to be capable of playing a major role in explaining religion.

Cognitive science is the study of the set of processes by means of which human beings come to know the world (Lawson, "Cognition," *Guide to the Study of Religion,* 2000). To the extent that religious knowledge counts as knowledge (and why should it not?) then whatever we have discovered about such processes certainly should be relevant to our study of religion. No one can deny that the contents of human minds are influenced by cultural processes. The issue is to describe and explain what is going on when our minds in their interaction with cultural phenomena create, employ, and transmit concepts of any kind including religious ones.

The emerging cognitive science of religion has focused on three problems: (1) How do human minds *represent* religious ideas? (2) How do human minds *acquire* religious ideas? (3) What forms of *action* do such ideas precipitate?

Religious Representations

Philosophers of religion, theologians, historians of religions, and even anthropologists of religion have sometimes argued that religious concepts are sufficiently different not only from each other but also from all other ideas to justify special analyses. Some such analyses have been conceived of in such radical terms that they have insisted that special experiences, special commitments, special methods, and even special mental spaces are required in order for religion to be understood. An alternative approach would be to show that *our ordinary, natural cognitive resources are sufficient to account for religious ideas*. In *Rethinking Religion: Connecting Cognition and Culture* (1990) Lawson and McCauley were able to show that such is the case for at least those religious representations about religious ritual action. That work argued that our cognitive resources for the representation of action were sufficient to account for the representation of religious ritual action.

Since that work, a great many further accomplishments in the cognitive study of religion have appeared. For example, Barrett and Keil (1996) showed experimentally that when people engaged in theological reflection (no matter which society they lived in), they tended to produce "theologically correct" formulations of the properties of their deities. However, when presented with stories of the gods and when being called upon to remember what they had been presented with, people tended to systematically mis-remember these properties of the gods. So, for example, while their theological thoughts of the gods represented them as being everywhere, nevertheless their recall of items in the story showed that they represented the gods as being in a specific location at a specific time. Evidently, human beings have deep intuitions about what agents are like. Agents are spatially and temporally bound. Even though peoples' theological reflections suggested rather unusual properties of a special class of agents, superhuman agents, nevertheless their ordinary intuitions overrode the contents of such abstract, "offline" reflections. One should not be surprised, therefore, that the gods are so frequently represented in anthropomorphic ways in religious narratives.

Pascal Boyer (1994) has further developed this notion of the use of our ordinary cognitive resources for religious representations by his groundbreaking work on intuitive ontologies. To have an intuitive ontology is simply to possess a set of expectations of what the world is like. In the terms of our intuitive ontologies, the world is a place where solid objects do not pass through each other, where living things require food to survive and grow, where animate things have goals, where agents have thoughts, and where artificial things do not come naturally—they have to be made. What Boyer has shown is that in order to have *religious* representations, these ordinary expectations about what the world is like only have to be *violated in minimal ways,* for example, either by violating only one of the assumptions of the ontological category involved or by transferring one of these assumptions from one category to another. Take, for example, the ontological category "person." Our ordinary expectations about persons are that they are intentional, biological, and physical agents. Violating only the physical assumptions about agents delivers the concept of a superhuman agent conceived of as intentional and living being but without a body.

Acquisition and Transmission

It is one thing to develop theories of how religious ideas are represented. It is another thing to account for how they are acquired. On the face of it, it would appear that, in the competition for ideas that make a difference to our understanding of the world, ideas about superhuman agents without bodies would hardly make the grade. Why have such preposterous (or, more gently, "counterintuitive") ideas not been eliminated a long time ago? Here, actually, is an area in which the cognitive science of religion has already made a contribution to cognitive science in general. What Boyer and others have been able to show is that in the processes of cultural transmission, counterintuitive ideas have a *mnemonic advantage*. In simple terms, ideas in which certain properties of our intuitive ontologies are violated *are more memorable than ideas which contain no such violations*. What Boyer has shown via the notion of a cognitive optimum is that in order for a religious idea to survive it requires two things. An idea needs to have the properties that any idea has, and it also needs something to make it stand out from competing ideas.

Now what we have learned from cognitive science is that the human mind acquires concepts in surprisingly complex ways. Developmental psychologists, for example, have shown that children actively construct their theories of what the world is like from the moment of birth. Rather than being blank slates which have information scribbled on them by the invisible hand of culture, children's minds show evidence of evolutionary design by their complex functional organization. Human minds have many competencies equipped to handle many domains of information. While, strictly speaking, there is no particular or special domain of religious information, human minds are so designed that they are responsive to certain kinds of information that capture human attention because of their memorability.

Religious Ritual Action

Lawson and McCauley (1990) have shown that the representation of religious ritual action depends upon quite ordinary action representations. The main thing that distinguishes religious ritual action representations from ordinary action representations is the assumption that some of the agents involved in the action possess special qualities. So, the basic action structure of a religious ritual is "someone does something to someone or something with a particular consequence and by means of a particular instrument." In order for such an ordinary action description to count as a ritual action description is to show that the agency involved possesses *special qualities*. Boyer's work about the minimal violations of intuitive ontological categories provides the means for explicating what makes such agents capable of being conceived of as superhuman agents. The special qualities of the agents presupposed in religious ritual action are that they violate some of the assumptions ordinarily associated with ordinary agents. But equally important, most of the properties of such agents, and the inferences that can be drawn from them are the properties and inferences that we would normally associate with any agent.

What we should also not miss about religious ritual representations is that they make it possible for certain things to get done that would not otherwise get done! The issues are not just ontological but also causal. Religious representations make it possible for people to devise special ways of bringing about new ways of associating with each other in social ways, hence the widespread practice of rites of passage. The big story is that cognitive scientists are beginning to unravel the mysteries involved in the cognitive processes which make such causal representations possible.

A cognitive science of religion is obviously still in the process of development. It has demonstrated its ability to encourage interdisciplinary work, for example, among anthropologists, psychologists, philosophers, computer scientists, and historians of religion. A new generation of scholars working in different disciplinary contexts are transgressing the boundaries of these disciplines and communicating with each other across those boundaries. Conferences involving cognition, culture, and religion are beginning to occur quite regularly and the proceedings of such conferences are rapidly moving toward publication (see, J. Andresen, *Religion in Mind*, [2001]) and a new journal, *The Journal of Cognition and Culture* (published by Brill Academic Publishers), will begin publication in 2001. The cognitive science of religion that is emerging promises to disclose aspects of human religions that, so far, have escaped explanation. Such explanations should find a warm welcome in the next generation of scholars of religion.

References

Andresen, J. (2001). *Religion in Mind*, Cambridge: Cambridge University Press.
Barrett, J. (2000). "Exploring the Natural Foundations of Religion," *Trends in Cognitive Sciences* 4 (1): 29–34.
Barrett, J., and F. Keil (1996). "Anthropomorphism and God Concepts: Conceptualizing a Non-Natural Entity," *Cognitive Psychology* 3: 219–47.
Boyer, P. (1994). *The Naturalness of Religious Ideas*, Berkeley: University of California Press.
Chomsky, N. (1957). *Syntactic Structures*, The Hague: Mouton.

Lawson, E. (1999). "Religious Ideas and Practices," in *MIT Encyclopedia for Cognitive Science*, 716–717, Cambridge, MA: MIT Press.

Lawson, E. (2000). "Cognition," in *Guide to the Study of Religion*, edited by W. Braun and R. McCutcheon, 338–49, London: Cassell.

Lawson, E., and R. McCauley (1990). *Rethinking Religion: Connecting Cognition and Culture*, Cambridge: Cambridge University Press.

McCauley, R. (1998). "Comparing the Cognitive Foundations of Religion and Science," Report # 37, Department of Psychology, Emory University, Atlanta, Georgia, 30322.

Pinker, S. (1994). *The Language Instinct: How the Mind Creates Language*, New York: William Morrow.

Sperber, D. (1975). *Rethinking Symbolism*, Cambridge: Cambridge University Press.

Sperber, D., and D. Wilson (1986). *Relevance: Communication and Cognition*, Cambridge, MA: Harvard University Press.

PART I

Theoretical Issues in the Cognitive Science of Religion

INTRODUCTION TO CHAPTER 2

In the last chapter, I pointed the way toward a cognitive science of religion. I hope that you were intrigued enough to take the project seriously, but I also hope that you might want to know more. The first thing you ought to know is that whenever a scholar moves out in a new direction, there are sure to be obstacles as well as opportunities that either slow down movement in that direction or speed it up. That is what this chapter is about: obstacles and opportunities.

2

Magic Bullets and Complex Theories

Magic bullets are wonderful things. They hit all targets simultaneously no matter how far apart. In the scientific study of any cultural phenomenon, whether it be religion, language, social structure, or political systems, we are easily tempted[1] to find that one bullet, that one idea, that will hit those targets and explain all of the phenomena in question. Here is a simple example. Let us begin an interview with an imaginary person by asking: How do children acquire a language? This imaginary person replies: Ah! Well, a language consists of a list of words, children hear people using words around them and are also taught words and so they slowly learn how those words are connected so they make sense, right? No problem! Magic bullet right on target! But wait, how do these young children distinguish noise from words? How do they acquire the criterion to make that distinction? How do they know how to arrange the words in a particular order that makes sense? In fact, there are scores of questions we can ask about language acquisition that are not answered by asserting that the child just needs to learn a list of words to acquire a language.

There are, of course, no scholars of human language that make such a simple claim, although I have asked this question of nonlinguistic scholars and I have received answers that are not too far from the "list of words" approach. Language acquisition works so smoothly that it is very easy to fail to recognize the astonishing achievement that it is. Linguists note that by the age of five years old, basic command of a language is already in place. Noam Chomsky in *Syntactic Structures* started a revolution in the study of language by showing how complicated the processes are that take place in this short time period and what it takes to bring them about (and with minimal instruction). That linguistic project, known as generative grammar, is still proceeding today with what is now known as minimalist theory in syntax and optimality theory in phonology. What is more, there are competing theoretical explorations in both fields that pursue even more alternative routes. We will attempt to show why the study of religion is just as complicated.

Much of what has gone on in the academic study of religion in the twentieth century is what Clifford Geertz called thick description that includes painstaking attention to detail while at the same time avoiding theoretical issues. The method also involves focusing on interpretation rather than explanation. In order to get the job done, for example, a scholar might decide to study religion by focusing on the continent of India. This may require the study of Sanskrit in order to be able to read prominent religious texts in the original language after which occurs the painstaking task of learning how to interpret those texts as well as placing them in their historical and sociocultural context. The temptation to find a magic bullet arises when the scholar tries to answer the question, "why do people imagine such interesting and seemingly bizarre ideas found in those Sanskrit texts?." With functional equipment in place, the scholar, having read Durkheim's *The Elementary Forms of Religious Life* in a sociology of religion class, may propose that "religion" functions as a social glue that binds people together. However, Edmund Leach, in his *Political Systems of Highland Burma,* showed how internally divisive religion can be. Exemplary in that regard is the study of "extreme" rituals (what I will refer to as *intense*). Such studies have shown that in some firewalking ceremonies, the hearts of relatives and friends of the firewalkers beat in synchrony with each other, whereas the hearts of spectators not related to the firewalkers did not. These researches would be the first to reject the claim that this experiment tells us all we need to know about religious ritual behavior. As McCauley and I demonstrate in *Bringing Ritual to Mind: Psychological Foundations of Cultural Forms,* rituals can be as boring as they can be intense. Noting the boring ones is as important, if not more so, in developing a coherent and scientific study of religious rituals as

MAGIC BULLETS AND COMPLEX THEORIES 25

examining the extreme ones. In fact, because they are not attention grabbing, they might very well be missed and, as a result, their role in a religious ritual system may be misunderstood. To be fair, it is highly unlikely they will actually be overlooked since rituals that we categorize as "boring" make up the vast majority of all ritual behaviors. But, like Williams James's so-called variety of religious experiences, more weight is often given to the most interesting phenomena and the result is often losing sight of the forest for the extreme trees, as it were (James 1902).

Let us take another example that highlights the distinction between (a) saying something and (b) doing something:

> Two people are walking along a path in Botswana having a conversation about the variety of acacia trees around.
>
> Suddenly one of them whispers urgently "There is a lion stalking us! We had better run like hell!"
>
> They run like hell.

We can clearly distinguish between the talking and the action. According to the theory of ritual competence, a similar distinction is very important when studying religious ritual which enables us to identify *ritual* speech and *ritual* action. In a particular religious ritual system, an example of ritual speech might be a prayer (aka ceremonial talking to a superhuman agent), whereas a ritual action might be either a ritual participant as (1) the subject of a superhuman agent's action or (2) the agent of an action in which the superhuman agent is the subject. An objector might ask: "what about speech acts?" One example is a judge saying to a defendant in a trial: "I now pronounce you guilty and your sentence is to serve twenty years in prison." However, the speech act represents the *decision* of the judge, whereas the action comes when the defendant is handcuffed and taken away.

The foregoing discussion is a microcosm of the complex myriad of components comprising the precise characterization of ritual behavior. But an important theoretical question looms on the horizon concerning the concept of "religion." We all too easily talk about it, which is why I have placed it in quotes. Both on the street and in the academy, everyone seems to know what "religion" is, courtesy of Wittgenstein and our collective intuitive and cultural repositories. Baptist, Buddhist, and Bahai all count as religions, right? But what makes them instances of the acquisition of a "religion" aside from the accident of birth, which is often controversial and tenuous? And why is this even important? One contribution of the cognitive science of "religion" has been to fractionate the subject matter.

For instance, many people consider the notion of a god to be fundamental to the practice of a religion. Stipulating this for the moment we must ask, "What is a god?" and how would such a concept emerge? Here is where cognitive/evolutionary science can step in. All human minds are equipped to entertain the concept of an agent for adaptive reasons. Agents are entities capable of intentional action. Psychologists who study cognitive development have shown that infants already know the difference between a person and a bedpost and even the difference between one person and a "mother person." They very early on, with remarkable speed, develop knowledge of the self, objects, and people (Rochat 2009). Just knowing the difference between a person and a physical object in the room is a process known as agency detection.[2]

It is not too long before a human baby can conceive of and develop a theory of mind of agents who are not physically present. The capacity for developing a theory of mind (ToM) plays a large role because to recognize another as an agent is to ascribe intentionality to them which includes the capacity to distinguish actions from events. Notice the fun game of hide and seek and how early the game can be played with infants. I have been told of a professor who, while in the birthing room when his baby was born, spontaneously stuck out his tongue at the baby. To his astonishment the baby responded by sticking its tongue out at him. At the very least this was an indication that the infant was capable of employing a whole number of cognitive processes, the underlying mechanisms of which are ready, very early on, to respond to play, to imaginative journeys, as well as to serious conundrums.

McCauley and I, in two of the books we wrote together, attempted, first, to connect cognition and culture by focusing on ritual behavior and, then, to show the philosophical foundation of cultural forms. In *Rethinking Religion*, we argued that the concept of superhuman agency and all of the conceptual machinery involved in correlated religious thought and behavior is a by-product of our amazing but standard cognitive machinery. As I've noted earlier, that machinery is in place very early in cognitive development and is available to underpin all kinds of behaviors. Therefore, the question "how does a person acquire a religion" is better addressed by asking, "How does one acquire the ability to think about agents, potential danger, actions, speech, intentionality, etc.?" In all of these cases, there is a short answer and a long answer. The short answer is: all the equipment is already in place and has been bequeathed to every member of *Homo sapiens sapiens* by the process of evolution. The long answer calls for a theory of how religious thought and the actions it informs are by-products of our standard tendencies, dispositions, and capacities.

A good example is our capacity to respond differently to imminent danger and potential danger (Boyer and Lienard 2006). An encounter with a predator immediately triggers the evolutionarily bequeathed (innate) fight, freeze, or flight responses. But we also live in a world of potential threats extant humans can anticipate; threats that resonate with those of the Paleolithic era: predation/assault, contamination/contagion, loss of resources, and detrimental changes in social status. It is not surprising then that evolution has prepared us to respond to such possibilities. Take the threats of predation/assault. Seeing a lion's footprints in the sand is a tenable sign of potential danger. One mitigating response is to walk carefully, perhaps along an alternate route. But if you live in a territory in which lions regularly roam, you need to be careful not only of signs of footprints but also of *anticipated* footprints. In other words, finding footprints in such regions is not only what triggers precaution systems but also the common knowledge of the ecology, in this case the prevalence of lions. This is a different sort of trigger and therefore requires a different precautionary measure such as doing something in advance of the journey. One possibility is a *cultural ritual* available in your repertoire: you make an offering to your god, patron saint of lions, or an òrìṣà that is linked to lions. Or perhaps you go to an herbalist who will provide you with the appropriate medicine for your purpose. While engaging in fieldwork in the *Mnweni* area of the Drakensberg Mountains in KwaZulu-Natal, South Africa, Joel Mort and I interviewed an *inyanga zemithi* who offered us *muthi* (medicine) to apply to our car which would render the car invisible to other drivers and therefore keep us safe on the long drive to Pietermaritzburg. Perhaps he also had muthi that would make a person invisible to lions should they be going out on a journey in lion infested territory. (There are, in fact, leopards in the Drakensberg Mountains!) If one arrives safely, the precautionary measure worked.[3] Looked at from an epidemiological approach, many similar rituals over time gravitate toward an attractor and reach some level of stability and become standard practice. From the perspective of neurobiology, human precautionary (or security motivation) systems produce "satiety signals," which provide the crucial internal sense that the precautionary measure taken was appropriate and successful.

All of this potentially, and ideally, leads to the integration of ritual competence, Sperberian attractors, precautionary repertoires, and security motivation theories, underlining the complexity of integrating theories and evidence as well as the crucial benefits of intertheoretical reducibility (Mort and Slone 2006; Fessler 2006). A good example of this effort is a workshop I co-organized with Joel Mort held in Stellenbosch, South Africa, in June 2009, bringing together social psychologists, psychiatrists, neurobiologists, anthropologists, evolutionary psychologists, zoologists, anthropologists, comparative religion scholars, and others resulting in a 2011 special issue of *Neuroscience and Biobehavioral Reviews* entitled "Threat-Detection and Precaution: Neuro-physiological, Behavioral, Cognitive and Psychiatric Aspects" (Szechtman and Boyer 2011). Crucially, "magic bullets" cannot be integrated with anything. They are essentially convenient heuristics that are often glamorized as explanations or even causal entities, a process which strips them of any heuristic benefit they might have had. They "remain intact and vague rather than fractionated and specified" (Mort and Slone 2006).

Notes

1 Both because of our intuitive cognitive architecture and because of the desire to identify the most parsimonious explanation. But as Peter Lipton, among others, have taught us, *parsimonious* is not a synonym of *simple*. (Lipton 1993).

2 See *The Infant's World* by Philippe Rochat to see how clever infants are and how we know that they are capable of differentiating between selves, objects, and people by means of habituation experiments.

3 See Szechtman and Woody "satiety signal."

References

Boyer, P., and P. Liénard (2006). "Why Ritualized Behavior? Precaution Systems and Action Parsing in Developmental, Pathological and Cultural Rituals," *Behavioral and Brain Sciences* 29: 1–56.

Boyer, P., and H. Szechtman, eds. (2011). "Threat-Detection and Precaution: Neuro-physiological, Behavioral, Cognitive and Psychiatric Aspects," *Neuroscience and Biobehavioral Reviews* 35 (4): 989–1080.

Fessler, D. M. (2006). "Contextual Features of Problem-Solving and Social Learning Give Rise to Spurious Associations, the Raw Materials for the Evolution of Rituals," *Behavioral and Brain Sciences* 29 (6): 617–18.

Geertz, C. (1973). *The Interpretation of Cultures*, vol. 5019, New York: Basic Books.

James, W. (1902). *The Varieties of Religious Experience: A Study in Human Nature*, New York: Longmans, Green, and Co.

Lawson, E. T., and R. N. McCauley (1993). *Rethinking Religion: Connecting Cognition and Culture*, Cambridge: Cambridge University Press.

Leach, E. R. (2021). *Political Systems of Highland Burma: A Study of Kachin Social Structure*, London: Routledge.

Lipton, P. (1993, January). "Is the Best Good Enough?" in *Proceedings of the Aristotelian Society*, vol. 93, 89–104, Aristotelian Society, Wiley.

McCauley, R. N., and E. T. Lawson (2002). *Bringing Ritual to Mind: Psychological Foundations of Cultural Forms*, Cambridge: Cambridge University Press.

Mort, J., and J. Slone (2006). "Considering the Rationality of Ritual Behavior," *Method & Theory in the Study of Religion* 18 (4): 424–39.

Rochat, P. (2009). *The Infant's World*, Cambridge, MA: Harvard University Press.

INTRODUCTION TO CHAPTER 3

While I was working my way to a doctoral degree in the Divinity School of the University of Chicago, a great deal of emphasis was placed on cooperation between the methods applied to various subject matters, so for example, religion and art, religious and the personality sciences, and social and theological ethics. The point was to encourage a dialogue between theologically grounded approach to study, and humanistic and scientific approaches. This was a very good idea and served me well when I lost interest in theology and began to slowly gravitate to more specifically humanistic and scientific approaches to human thought and behavior. In this section, I reflect on some of the issues that arise when one adopts an interdisciplinary approach in their studies.

3

The Wedding of Psychology, Ethnography, and History

Methodological Bigamy or Tripartite Free Love?

Some years ago, I was adventurous enough to suggest that cognitive science was relevant to the study of history (Lawson 1994). Much to my surprise and pleasure, I received very positive and encouraging responses from historians and, in fact, was invited to make my case in a graduate seminar offered by the history department at my own university. My rather simple, if not simple-minded, claim was that, if historians and other social scientists were willing to make claims about the transmission of traditions, then it would also be their job to help the rest of us identify the mechanisms that underwrite the processes of transmission.

Since the publication of this article, two books have been published that demonstrate willingness on the part of social scientists with a historical interest to do something like that. I refer to Harvey Whitehouse's *Arguments and Icons: Divergent Modes of Religiosity* (2000) and Steven Mithen's *The Prehistory of the Mind* (1996). In Whitehouse's work, we find a sophisticated wedding of cognitive psychology, ethnography, and history. In Mithen's work, we find a powerful argument about how archaeology can not only be informed by cognitive psychology but can, in turn, on the basis of information derived from archaeological research, make a fundamental contribution to our understanding of the working of the human mind.

These two volumes are genuinely interdisciplinary endeavors leading to coherent and compelling arguments about the origin, structure, and transmission of religious thought and practice. In the case of Mithen, the claim is clear: we can only understand the present by knowing the past. In the long run, this means gathering together everything we know about cognitive development, not only ontogenetically but also through our knowledge of the evolutionary history of the mind, in order to relate the past to the present. Mithen has effectively accomplished the transformation of archaeology from a theoretical and empirical perspective on the past to a science of the mind in a historical perspective thoroughly informed by evolutionary, cognitive, and developmental psychology.

The work of Harvey Whitehouse is equally ambitious. While pivotally ethnographic, his work is deeply sensitive both to psychological processes, particularly those that are mnemonic, and to historical facts. I do not know what historians and ethnographers make of his arguments, but I do know that those of us who are developing the cognitive science of religion have been persuaded about the importance of his insights, especially as these involve issues of the transmission of cultural forms.

The works of both Mithen and Whitehouse are scintillating examples of what I have jokingly called tripartite free love rather than methodological bigamy. Bigamy is a triangular relationship in which at the apex of the triangle is the bigamist and at the base of the triangle are the objects of bigamy. Essential to this triangular relationship is that the one member at the base is ignorant of the existence of the other member at the base. This ignorance spells trouble in the short or long run when the bigamy is discovered. And the consequent knowledge typically alienates all concerned.

In tripartite free love, each member of the relationship knows about the other. This does not necessarily spell trouble as long as mutual respect is present. However, the danger of subservience always looms. I do not want to overplay this metaphor because of its titillating character. The point I wish to make is that whether one is a psychologist, an anthropologist, or a historian, one has work to do that is respectively psychological, ethnographic, and historical. The virtual autonomy of those researchers grants them freedom to do what they do best while, of course, looking at what is going on in closely related disciplines. Their autonomy is qualified by their dependence on information generated by the practice of the other disciplines in the triangle.

A perusal of the indexes of the relevant journals demonstrates that the practitioners of these disciplines know when their work reflects the particular perspectives typical of their particular discipline and when their work creatively transgresses boundaries. One would not expect to find a discussion of historical questions, such as whether Caesar crossed the Rubicon, in a psychology or anthropology journal. Nevertheless, there are crucial moments in which the question of whether Caesar crossed the Rubicon is a psychological and ethnographic, and not simply a historical, problem. It is a psychological problem in the sense that whether the event is either remembered or imagined, and therefore communicated horizontally and vertically, depends upon its ability to command attention. Claims to historical knowledge presuppose mnemonic facts. It is also an ethnographic problem in the sense that this putative event plays a role in the lore of the traditions of the society in which it is remembered, discussed, and propagated. Claims to ethnographic knowledge all presuppose mnemonic processes. So, it is at that interdisciplinary moment that a wedding of perspectives between the three disciplines involved, freely entered into and with due respect for the integrity of each, is required.

Of course, this is also exactly the point at which methodological concerns arise. Is the historian, for example, knowledgeable enough about either psychology or ethnography to support his or her theoretical maneuvers? Is the ethnographer who appeals to mnemonic facts not guilty of reducing social facts to psychological facts? Charges of reductionism arise because it is inevitable that someone will ask which level of explanation is fundamental and which derivative.

Reductionism involves a relationship between different types and levels of theories. Sometimes theories of one kind can be reduced to better theories at the same level. So, for example, psychological theories that focus only on environmental variables might be capable of being reduced to theories that include internal variables such as cognitive states, which transform the external variables in novel, interesting, and predictable ways. Sometimes, of course, theories at one level of explanation can be reduced to theories at a deeper level. So, for example, psychological theories that focus on mental states might be capable of being reduced to nothing but brain states. I do not think that the relationships between psychology, history, and ethnography have been sufficiently clarified to decide yet whether ethnography and history (putatively higher-level theoretical matrices) are grist for reduction to purely psychological categories. This is not to say that the facts that ethnographers and historians' traffic in do not have psychological foundations (which I think they do). There is, however, a big difference between saying that cultural facts have psychological foundations and claiming that cultural facts are nothing but the foundations. There is always more to a building than its foundations. There may be more than one floor to the mansion, but good architectural design encourages the easy and efficient flow of traffic throughout the building.

Therefore, I want to claim that it will be possible for some considerable time to come to have a free, loving, and committed relationship (to revert to my metaphor) between psychology, ethnography, and history (including its archaeological dimensions), at least at crucial moments. The test of this claim is whether a coherent set of theoretical proposals that attend to psychological, ethnographic, and historical processes can be substantiated by logical analysis and empirical and experimental evidence. The playing field between these disciplines is still level. In fact, the interdisciplinary character of the modes project depends upon conceiving of the players as being not only on the same turf but in the same game. Interdisciplinary projects can lead to the establishment of new disciplines.

A prime candidate for such an interdisciplinary theory that combines the insights of psychology, ethnography, and history is the work of Harvey Whitehouse. Whitehouse's postulation of doctrinal and imagistic modes of religiosity provides important heuristic tools for unpacking some of the critical features informing the trajectory of religious change and development. In short, with this perspective, it is possible for us to understand more deeply the processes of the transmission of both concepts and practices not only horizontally but also vertically. Whitehouse has made a fundamental epidemiological contribution to the factors involved in the spread of religion across cultures and through time.

Such heuristic tools not only enable us to develop an explanatory understanding of the contents of our history books about the successes and failures of religious institutions but also open up new avenues of investigation in fieldwork. Furthermore, by focusing upon ritual practices and not just upon religious ideas, Whitehouse brings an observable and empirical dimension to theoretical claims about cognitive processes.

While the initial claims that Whitehouse makes involve a small geographical area, they enable the theoretician to examine the possibility of making claims about other geographical areas and ultimately about proposing cross-cultural and historical generalizations.

PSYCHOLOGY, ETHNOGRAPHY, AND HISTORY

In any such project, there is always the chance that important ideas will be missed. I think that participants in the modes project inspired by the theorizing of Whitehouse need to take additional theoretical perspectives and the empirical and theoretical work that accompanies them into account. The first of these is the psychological studies on theological correctness by Justin Barrett and Frank Keil (1996) and later Barrett (2000). Such work should be synthesized with the ideas entertained in the modes project because it is clear that the doctrinal mode is infused with theological correctness and, as such, has implications for the processes of cultural transmission. These studies also point to the fact that offline reflective thinking is difficult to transmit, even when the necessary institutions are established to perpetuate these modes of thought. Theology is not easy to come by.

The second of these is Pascal Boyer's (2001) work on intuitive ontology, which is important because it focuses upon the kinds of templates that typically underwrite our variable concepts and have, therefore, a significant impact on our explanatory understanding of the processes of acquiring and transmitting information within and across cultures and through the historical process.

The third of these has to do with the notion of balanced and unbalanced religions and the role that conceptual control plays in the evolution of religious systems in general and religious ritual systems in particular. Robert McCauley and I have tried to show that a small number of variables exert selection pressures on all religious ritual systems and how these systems meet the mnemonic and motivational demands necessary for their transmission (McCauley and Lawson 2002). The interdisciplinary study of religion, infused with the insights provided by psychology, ethnography, and history, is opening up new avenues of knowledge that promise to expand our understanding of human thought and behavior in interesting new ways. Such a wedding should provide a welcome sense of pageantry to those participants eager to enjoy the party.

References

Barrett, Justin L. (2000). "Exploring the Natural Foundations of Religion," *Trends in Cognitive Science* 4: 29–34.

Barrett, Justin L., and Frank Keil (1996). "Conceptualizing a Non-natural Entity: Anthropomorphism in God Concepts," *Cognitive Psychology* 31: 219–47.

Boyer, Pascal (2001). *Religion Explained: The Evolutionary Origins of Religious Thought,* New York: Basic Books.

Lawson, E. Thomas (1994). "Counterintuitive Notions and the Problem of Transmission: The Relevance of Cognitive Science for the Study of History," *Historical Reflections/ Réflexions Historique* 20 (3): 481–95.

McCauley, Robert N., and E. Thomas Lawson (2002). *Bringing Ritual to Mind: Psychological Foundations of Cultural Forms*, Cambridge: Cambridge University Press.

Mithen, Steven (1996). *The Prehistory of the Mind: The Cognitive Origins of Art, Religion, and Science*, London: Thames and Hudson.

Whitehouse, Harvey (2000). *Arguments and Icons: Divergent Modes of Religiosity*, Oxford: Oxford University Press.

INTRODUCTION TO CHAPTER 4

In the autumn of 1990, I was invited by Pascal Boyer to spend some time at Cambridge University; Rethinking Religion had just been published and Pascal was working on issues raised by that book in a book of his own, soon to be published as The Naturalness of Religious Ideas. *A consequence of that visit was an invitation by Pascal to contribute to an anthology,* Cognitive Aspects of Religious Symbolism. *This is the essay I wrote for that volume. It represents my first attempt to describe some important aspects of* Rethinking Religion: Connecting Cognition and Culture, *particularly issues in the acquisition of knowledge. It also solidified a friendship that has lasted to this day.*

4

Cognitive Categories, Cultural Forms, and Ritual Structures

Introduction

The recognition that human beings learn more than they are taught, already prefigured quite early in the Platonic literature and much later in Kant's notion of the synthetic a priori, continues to intrigue scholars concerned with cognitive matters, especially those with a stake in the possible impact of the cognitive sciences on culture theory. In fact, much to the dismay of empiricists, it has breathed new life into the rationalist tradition. Possessing more knowledge than instruction can account for obviously presents a puzzle worth solving.

Among cognitive theoreticians (especially in generative linguistics and cognitive anthropology), the acquisition puzzle has given rise to a range of suggested solutions. At one end of the theoretical spectrum proponents of the autonomy of cultural systems postulate the presence and operation of very subtle and hidden cultural forces silently transmitting culturally constrained cognitive knowledge from a "cultural system" to the largely "empty" minds of cultural participants. At the other end of the spectrum nativists proffer innate cognitive mechanisms, replete with cognitive content, as solutions to "the discrepancy problem." Even theorists in the middle seem willing to nudge the direction of research in one direction rather than the other.

There can be little doubt that arguments about acquisition take place in contentious territory. The issues are by no means resolved. Proof of that lies in the continuing combat between non-nativists and nativists about the significance of, and the solutions to, the noted discrepancy between the amount of cultural knowledge by explicit tuition and the actual knowledge a person in that culture possesses as well as about the most adequate explanatory models capable of accounting for the discrepancy. Various forms of cultural and biological determinism wait anxiously in the wings for the chance to enact familiar roles in new plays.

From my point of view, what is at stake in this debate about the acquisition of cultural knowledge is not only the issue about the nature and status of the mechanisms of acquisition but also the issue about what counts as knowledge. After all, you had better have a theory of *what* it is that is acquired in such a puzzling fashion if you are going to argue about *how* what is acquired is in fact acquired. In this case at least, questions of form prove inseparable from questions of origin.

In this chapter, I confront the acquisition problem in a relatively oblique manner. I argue that a theory of religious ritual action which employs the strategy of competence theorizing is capable of illuminating certain aspects of the acquisition debate in the very process of laying the groundwork for an explanation of religious ritual. The theory I discuss here in outline was initially presented by Robert McCauley and me in *Rethinking Religion: Connecting Cognition and Culture* (Lawson and McCauley 1990) and can be found there in a larger framework. I intend here, therefore, only to highlight some of the key features of our theory and to address some of its consequences, especially those having to do with the acquisition problem.

In this chapter, I discuss, first, agreements and disagreements among theorists about the acquisition of knowledge. Then I suggest that competence theorizing provides a fruitful approach to those phenomena (such as religious ritual), which straddle the cognitive-cultural divide. Following that, I narrow the focus by defending theorizing about the representation of religious ritual action rather than religious thought. Having thus set the stage, I then present in brief compass the theory of religious ritual action which McCauley and I have developed. I show that our theory contains three elements: (1) an abstract mechanism for the generation of representations of religious ritual action, (2) a conceptual scheme which affects the operation of the mechanism, and (3) a set of universal principles which are activated by the application of the conceptual scheme to the action-representation system and which constrain the representation of religious ritual action. Finally, I discuss the consequences of our theory for the problem of the acquisition of knowledge.

Underdetermination and the Acquisition of Knowledge

When dealing with contentious matters, it is all too easy to miss fundamental areas of agreement among opponents. Differences are usually easier to take note of than similarities. This is especially the case with the acquisition problem. For example, few scholars would deny the fact of the obvious mastery of cultural form people exhibit in their *linguistic* traffic with each other. Talking comes naturally.[1] Nor would many investigators disagree about the ease with which people inhabit their *customary* worlds. People are remarkably adept in knowing what counts as a customary act and what particular kind of act is appropriate to the situation in question. Nor would many scholars raise serious doubts about the dexterity cultural participants display in their judgments about well-formedness in *symbolic* systems. The data produced by anthropological fieldwork would be uninteresting were it to lack the expertise which all members of a culture possess and which they display whenever anthropologists elicit judgments about the form and content of their social and cultural life. In fact, respect for, and attention to, the judgments informants make about their symbolic behavior is a necessary condition for engaging in fieldwork.

With regard to linguistic, customary, and symbolic matters, therefore, most cultural theorists would readily acknowledge that people daily demonstrate their cultural competence. People know what to think about their cultural world, and, for the most part, how to act in it. The problem lies in explaining such mastery. It is here that disagreements emerge most sharply. Indeed, these disagreements extend beyond the *fact* of mastery to questions about which *mechanisms* are capable of accounting for it.

Competence theorizing about cultural phenomena arose as a method for dealing with such problems in the specific field of linguistic theory. And it has had considerable success. (In fact, some theoreticians argue that it is the only game in town.) Its success in the study of language suggests its considerable promise in the analysis of other cultural phenomena, especially the domain of religious ritual.

Competence Theories

Competence theorists employ a thoroughly psychological strategy for dealing with cultural phenomena. They demonstrate the viability of cognitive categories for the analysis of cultural forms. While methodological solipsism is not a necessary condition for competence theorizing, competence theorists do not hesitate to hold in abeyance judgments about the physical realization of the principles they propose. They are, however, unwilling to assume that cultures are autonomous systems, which unproblematically transmit cultural information through mysterious channels to cultural participants. Their cognitivist tactics require no precipitous leaps either to cultural systems or biological structures, although they are willing to consider significant roles for biological and cultural systems at later stages of analysis.

From a competence point of view, cultural systems are not simply producers of knowledge, they are also products of cognitive mechanisms and structures. Of particular interest to competence theorists are the judgments people make about cultural forms. These judgments provide a readily available source of data capable of considerable theoretical manipulation.

Competence theorists are particularly eager to avoid cultural tourism. They are not convinced that mere exposure to alien cultural spheres with their vast array of cultural facts will ensure access to a cultural "system" underlying the welter of cultural detail. Competence theorists prefer instead to start at the cognitive level by identifying the mastery that cultural participants possess of the culture in which "they live and move and have their being." Such a move sets competence theorizing apart from classical anthropology, which has often seemed content to assume that mere exposure to cultural phenomena is a sufficient condition for the generation of knowledge about such phenomena.

The competence approach involves constructing testable and more realistic models of what is "in the heads" of cultural participants than empty slates or general learning mechanisms. Their view is that competence models provide, albeit quite abstractly, a more adequate way of viewing cognitive transactions among people in their traffic with their cultural context. The models also provide access to a level of psychological systematicity that is empirically tractable.

A more adequate view involves showing that, in order for people to participate in an efficient and unimpeded manner in social life, they require cultural competence (whether or not they are aware of possessing such knowledge). "Participating in an efficient and unimpeded manner in social life" means (1) having the ability to form adequate judgments about the *well-formedness* of cultural practices, (2) possessing the capacity to make judgments about the *relationships* among practices, and (3) being able to understand the relationship of particular sets of practices to the larger aggregate of practices characteristic of a cultural form as a whole.

I think that whatever systematicity exists at the level of culture itself is already contained and reflected in the cognitive structures theoretically available to the investigator at the psychological level of analysis. The point here is that rather than culture providing the explanatory categories for human behavior culture is itself at least partially in need of explanation by noncultural, that is cognitive, categories. This cognitivist view has been reinforced by a long tradition in the philosophy of social science critical of the ability of the concept of culture to bear the explanatory weight that some social scientists have attempted to accord it.

In the move from exclusively cultural to predominantly cognitive categories, competence theory adopts the standard scientific strategy of idealization in the explanation of cultural phenomena. Such a maneuver involves focusing upon abstracted general properties and suspending certain details in order to construct theoretical models of mind capable of representing some aspect of cultural competence.

The purpose of constructing such "artificial minds" or "artificial knowledge modules" lies in devising means for discovering whether the principles, processes, and products defined by the model are capable of accounting for the judgments made by ideal cultural participants (who provide the subject matter for the model) about the form and content of the cultural activity in which they participate. Ultimately, we would expect a model worth its salt to be capable of demonstrating that the products generated by the underlying principles would conform, however indirectly, to the actual judgments made by the participants—although there is many a slip between the competence cup and the performance lip.

Theorizing about Ritual Competence

Religious rituals are instances of symbolic behavior. Competence theorizing suggests techniques for their analysis. The theoretical object of such analysis consists of representations in the minds of ideal ritual participants. Because they are *cognitive* representations and thus not directly accessible, the data employed in their analysis consist of peoples' *judgments* about ritual form. By "symbolic" I refer to those phenomena which are culturally uncodified in the main, restricted in their use and transmission, and, though ubiquitous in social and personal representations, seldom explicitly taught (Lawson and McCauley 1990: 2–3). Their theoretical interest lies in the fact that they are phenomena over which participants in a culture show considerable mastery without having been explicitly taught. They are instances of symbolic fluency. As such they raise questions about acquisition because in making such "informed" judgments people demonstrate that they know more than they were taught. Ethnographers who have concerned themselves with the issue note the very haphazard, unsystematic, and partial role that instruction plays in cognitive development.

What is fortunate for competence theorists interested in religious ritual representation and the issues which emerge from it is that they do not have to start their analyses of such symbolic-cultural phenomena de novo. Generative linguists have already spent a considerable amount of energy in the last thirty years developing and perfecting various formal techniques for the analysis of language, the cultural "system" par excellence. They have provided useful, empirically tractable methods consisting of a wide range of skillfully honed formal tools capable of analyzing apparently unruly cultural phenomena in productive ways. Because the systems of rules and representations constructed by generative linguists have proved themselves to be powerful techniques in the study of language, we think that they promise to be transportable to other areas of cognitive inquiry. They have considerable heuristic value in analyzing patterns of representations.

Of particular interest to those of us concerned with religious ritual is the fact that these formal strategies produced in the competence-theoretic approach to linguistic phenomena have proved remarkably successful not only in the analysis of the grammars of particular natural languages but in explanatory theorizing about universal principles that underlie and constrain particular grammars. In other words, participants in competence-theoretic research have made progress in showing how a small set of universal principles is capable of constraining a larger set of formal systems.

Such techniques have great heuristic value for the study of religious ritual, especially when such study crosses cultural boundaries in search of cultural commonalities at whatever level such generality may be found. The overall competence approach provides rich resources for the study of symbolic-cultural phenomena such as ritual. These resources should not be taken lightly.

Despite the tendency of the anthropological tradition of inquiry to overemphasize cultural *systems* from a noncognitive perspective, the clues provided by the science of language suggest that language and ritual have much in common. Like language, ritual systems transgress cognitive and sociocultural lines of demarcation by showing that a purely cultural analysis is never enough. In fact, it becomes clear that ritual systems straddle fences and join territories, which classical approaches to cultural phenomena have insisted upon holding apart (by claiming autonomy for social and cultural systems, *a la* Durkheim). Despite such claims of autonomy (and even methodological solipsism), it has become increasingly evident that both religious ritual and language require in their explanation a reference to, and an ordering of, the relationships between sociocultural and psychological variables. Further, it can no longer be taken at face value that cultural categories have methodological primacy in analyzing cultural phenomena. In fact, significant progress is being made in the analysis of cultural phenomena by commencing with cognitive structures which then lead to questions about cultural forces and innate structures. This is what I meant by saying earlier that even those in the middle of the spectrum are willing to nudge the direction of research in one direction or the other.

Ritual Action and Religious Thought

The competence-theoretic approach McCauley and I employ focuses upon the representation of religious *ritual action* rather than the more inclusive domain of religious *thought* or religious *ideas*. We do so because we see a significant opportunity for explaining important features of religion by choosing a narrower focus. For one thing, analyzing the representation of ritual action provides more opportunities for specifying structural elements than is possible at the more inclusive level of thought. Of course, I do not mean to imply that McCauley and I are uninterested in religious ideas. In fact, *conceptual schemes* play a significant role in our theory by providing conceptual content to the system of rules which generate abstract ritual structures in the system for the representation of action which we propose.

We have chosen, therefore, to theorize about the cognitive representation of action systems that ritual participants employ in their judgments about the form of their ritual systems rather than the more inclusive ontologies that constrain their thinking. This shift of cognitive attention from religious ideas to the representation of action in particular permits a generative strategy that is much more difficult to achieve at more inclusive levels of ideational analysis.

I do not mean to imply that religious ontologies are unconstrained. Boyer (1990) argues that religious ontologies are constrained by universal cognitive mechanisms. In fact, Boyer has shown how core ideas affect and are presupposed by religious ideas. However, I think that there lies a more structured level for analysis in religious ritual action than is available in the variability characteristic of religious thought in a particular culture. Dan Sperber, for example, has shown how "creative" the interpretative abilities of religious participants are in their symbolic traffic with each other, with the social world they inhabit, and with the fieldworker in search of cultural information (1975). As I have already stated, then, we do not intend to ignore religious thought; in our theory, we make a special place for religious conceptual schemes as providing the *content* required by ritual structures. But the pursuit of form is by no means a fruitless task.

We do wish, especially, to counteract a tendency among scholars interested in religion, *particularly philosophers of religion,* to overemphasize the role that religious beliefs play in the interpretation and explanation of religion. Particularly troubling is their overattentiveness to consciously entertained *beliefs* and their putative role in religious life. The literature on "propositional attitudes" is vast. Some philosophers of religion even talk as though religious life were nothing more than a set of bizarre beliefs in need only of translation, rationalization, or refutation. And some anthropologists have fueled these fires. They have given comfort to and aided and abetted these tendencies in quite specific ways. For example, intellectualists, symbolists, and functionalists jointly conspire to explain away religious thought by employing concepts such as "idiomatic difference," "cryptic meaning," and "social integration" rather than seeing through the apparent bizarreness of religious thought to the ordinariness of the underlying cognitive structures, especially as these are evident in the representation of religious ritual action.

While we concede that in some general sense ritual participants do have "theories" of the world (and often more than one at the same time!), it is an intellectualist mistake to overemphasize the role that intellectual curiosity plays in daily life. The recovery of the mundane underlying the bizarre would be a major leap forward in theoretical work. Boyer has made that leap. In his discussion of constraints upon religious thought, Boyer argues that some important properties of religious ideas are the outcome of quite ordinary cognitive processes which structure everyday, nonreligious aspects of experience. Among these, for example, are views of causality that do not differ remarkably in religious and nonreligious contexts. I agree. What Boyer has accomplished is to show that religious thought is not nearly as bizarre as it is sometimes taken to be. Rather than contradicting Boyer's analysis, the theory of ritual action that McCauley and I propose reinforces it.

My point is that ritual participants do not only have beliefs about the world (the problem of reference), nor are they satisfied simply to categorize its levels (the problem of ontology). They also cognitively *organize* it in such a way that they can *act* in it (the problem of action). And they do so in marvelously structured ways most of which are quite tacit. We cannot, however, be content to settle for an analysis of religion in general and religious ritual action in particular that stops with having identified the categories people employ in their traffic with their world.

One undesirable consequence of focusing upon bizarreness as the fundamental characteristic of religious beliefs is becoming embroiled by the distractions of arguments about the conditions under which apparently bizarre beliefs can be taken to be true or false, declared to be meaningless, or be justified only "psychologically," that is, by their functions. Actually, in explanatory theorizing about religious ritual behavior, very little hangs on whether religious concepts are true or false, whether they have a reference, or even whether they fulfill needs of some kind or other. Rather, what counts is their cognitive availability not only for a "naming of parts" but for providing shape and meaning to the variability of daily social life. More than classification is at stake because daily life is filled with "traditional repetition" (Boyer 1990). I think that what underlies such "traditional repetition" provides a productive domain for explanatory theorizing. It *will* show us that people have both basic and peripheral categories. It will also show us that people act in quite structured ways in their social life.

So, granting that universal cognitive mechanisms constrain religious thought, we still have an interesting opportunity for productive analysis at the level of the representation of ritual action. And at that level of analysis, it is the case that the representation of ritual action, rather than being a completely anomalous sphere, is constrained by the representation of action generally. McCauley and I argue (1991: 158) that quite ordinary assumptions about action constrain the representation of religious ritual action. No matter how unusual a religion's metaphysical assumptions about the entities that populate the world may be, the ritual system will provide a means for ensuring that religious ritual representations respect the general logical distinctions which inform an everyday view of action.

A Theory of the Representation of Religious Ritual

Our theory has two goals. The first of these is to provide a clear and efficient way for describing the cognitive representation of religious ritual action. The second of these is to make predictions about important features of religious rituals so represented. Our theory consists of the following:

1. A *system for the representation of action.* This "action-representation system" consists of a set of rules and categories which generate abstract structural descriptions for the representation of ritual form.

2. A *conceptual scheme.* This scheme, which contains semantic information, activates the set of universal principles and penetrates the action-representation system.

3. A *set of universal principles.* These principles constrain the products of the action-representation system and feedback the results into the conceptual scheme.

I shall discuss these three aspects of our theory in turn.

The Representation of Ritual Action

Though our theory consists of a system for the representation of religious ritual action we wish to emphasize that the representation of religious ritual action differs in only very minor ways from the representation of any action.[2] In other words, the representation of religious ritual action is just a special case of the representation of human action generally. So whatever set of rules we devise to generate descriptions of the representation of religious ritual action will differ only in minor ways from those designed to generate descriptions of ordinary actions. For example, taking a sip of wine from a glass is a case of human action capable of being cognitively represented by the concepts applicable to any standard feature of daily life, namely, the categories of agents, actions, and objects. (Agents pick up glasses, open mouths, and swallow liquids.)

Taking a sip of wine from a chalice held by a priest in the ritual of the mass involves *additional descriptive elements*; it does not, however, entail accessing new categories for an adequate description of the ritual beyond the initial level already available in the representation of any action. This means that ritual representation involves elements which are merely special cases of agents, actions, and objects: priests filling chalices with wine, priests consecrating wine, priests and parishioners drinking consecrated wine, priests chanting sentences over wine so consecrated, and, at embedded levels of description, superhuman agents ordaining priests who, in turn, consecrate wine and ritually encourage parishioners to drink it.

The presence of such semantic information (provided by the conceptual scheme) in the representation of the action enables us to distinguish between action in general and religious action in particular. Thus, declaring the wine in the chalice to be the blood of Jesus Christ spilled for the ritual participant's sins, and drinking the wine so declared from a suitable chalice, involves little more than special descriptions of the agents, actions, and objects involved. Maintaining one overall formal description of action discourages tampering with standard ontological assumptions that people possess in any society and which they competently employ in their representations of action. We still have agents (with some special properties) acting (in special ways) upon objects (with some special features). It also shows that there is a continuity between religious representations and representations generally. The most significant additional element present in the cognitive representation of religious ritual is the presumption of superhuman agency on the part of ritual participants. (I shall return to a discussion of superhuman agency later.)

As I have already promised earlier, the formalism McCauley and I employ in the representation of religious ritual action is very similar to that employed in generative linguistics (Lawson and McCauley 1990: 84–136). Our scheme for the representation of action involves two components, a formation system and an object agency filter. The formation system consists of formation rules and constituents. The constituents consist of action elements and category symbols. The formation rules generate initial structural descriptions in which the category symbols are instantiated by action elements. The initial structural descriptions generated by the formation rules are constrained by an object agency filter, which ensures the proper classification of agents and, in those situations where the formal system generates objects in the role of agents, either rearranges the initial structural description or eliminates it. For example, a priest is an agent, drinking is an act, and wine is an object. The rules that McCauley and I have proposed initially permit not only descriptions of priests drinking wine (agents acting upon objects) but also permit wine to consecrate ritual participants (objects acting as agents upon objects). In this latter instance, we clearly have a situation in which common sense assumptions are violated. This is an infelicitous result not only in our ordinary understanding of action but in some sense in religious understandings as well. The object agency filter is a principle which either eliminates such infelicitous descriptions (in which objects assume the role of agents acting upon objects, for example, wine consecrating ritual participants) or rearranges the description. For example, the object agency filter permits a redescription in which a permissible agent, a parishioner, consecrates herself *by means of* drinking consecrated wine.[3]

Such a generative scheme permits structural descriptions of an indefinitely large set of religious rituals and permits us to identify important features of ritual systems, but the products of such a scheme by itself would hardly hold most theoreticians' interest for very long. For one thing, it's abstract structures Jack content. But we promise something more interesting than a radically syntactic approach; we argue that the conceptual scheme provides the mechanism which supplies the content. The semantic and the syntactic elements are inextricably meshed. I turn next to a discussion of the semantic component.

The Conceptual Scheme and the Religious Conceptual Scheme

The scheme that is represented in the minds of ritual participants in any society is that set of concepts the effects of which are made manifest in cultural phenomena such as the following:

1   narrative, either oral or written, which are always in the process of change, alteration, emendation, and even elimination;

46 IMAGING THE COGNITIVE SCIENCE OF RELIGION

2 commentaries on, and interpretations of, these narratives;

3 abstract analyses and reflections, practiced by special groups but usually accessible to everyone;

4 prescriptions and instructions about procedures to be enacted, obligations to be met, norms to be conformed to, and criteria to be followed, all of which may be preserved in either oral or written form in narratives, commentaries, manuals, etc.;

5 calendrical orders (what happens when);

6 spatial organization (who does what where);

7 social relations (who does what to whom, or is permitted to do so); and

8 systems of classification of the personal, social, and natural worlds.

While these cultural phenomena are available to the cultural participant, the conceptual scheme is not consciously accessible. In fact, the theoretician infers it from the judgments made by the cultural participants about their ritual system. The concepts in the scheme assume religious content at the moment that they implicate the action of superhuman agents at some level of structural description. Without such a pivotal concept, it makes little sense to think that even a vague area of theoretical interest deserves explanatory treatment. So modified by this pivotal notion, a conceptual scheme has a number of systematic functions (Lawson and McCauley 1990: 157): (1) it addresses questions about the meaning of religious rituals; (2) it contains accounts of where, how, and why rituals originated; (3) it explicates why rituals have many of the features that they do; and (4) it provides reasons for what they intend to accomplish. In addition, the conceptual system contains information about eligible participants and will even specify who qualifies as eligible substitutes. As we shall see later, it also makes the acquisition problem more binding.

One of the seductive features of conceptual schemes for theoreticians is how easily analyzable they sometimes appear to be. They can rather quickly become the exclusive focus of attention. As I have already argued against the philosophers of religion, placing an undue emphasis upon conceptual schemes tempts the inquirer to become more interested in their truth content than in their structural role in a religious system. Concentrating on conceptual schemes (to the exclusion of religious ritual action) also places more emphasis upon what is *publicly* available than is warranted: for example, when encountering polite strangers asking questions about everyday life, people in other societies are usually quite ready to tell a story, give directions, explicate customs, identify important dates, describe kin relationships, clarify procedures, and so on. Even when voluble informants are not available to the polite and inquisitive strangers, some cultures have books and documents available which provide reams of information. And in those societies which transmit their traditions orally the various keepers of the oral tradition are often approachable (if not always willing) to dispense the desired information to persistent and courteous inquire.

What is stored in public representations, however, is not necessarily identical with the conceptual system that is actually represented in the heads of ritual participants, especially when such a conceptual system has very complex cognitive relationships to other cognitive systems. In fact, even the public information often presupposes hidden cognitive structures which only adequate theory can bring to light.

First, there will be much information, especially very esoteric information, in the overall public representations of a society that is not available to all ritual participants. If it is inaccessible, then it becomes problematic about showing how it has influenced individual conceptual systems. We need a special argument about the transmission of information to make any case at all. Second, there will be things going on in the heads of participants from a cognitive-theoretic point of view that can be found nowhere in the public representations. Some representation or other will always be available for the ritual participants, but the set as a whole will never be necessary for providing any particular ritual action with specific content. The reason for this is that once ritual participants have the (tacit) system in hand (or in the head!) then those ritual participants are ritually competent to make judgments about their ritual practices because they have internalized a formation system of some kind. The internalized system is doing the explanatory work.

Once the "grammar" of ritual has been internalized, the ritual participant knows how to employ the system in daily life. There is a great deal of information in the public set of representations that is simply not necessary for such employment; for example, the ritual participant might be quite capable of making judgments about eligible participants without having to know the contents of some esoteric doctrine held by a special priesthood. Further, both the public store of information *and* the secret doctrines known only by the few sometimes lag behind the religious ritual system that is actually in place in the ritual participant's mind. We used to refer to this as "cultural lag." Competence theorizing puts a positive twist on an acknowledged phenomenon.

The conceptual scheme (understood now not just as the cultural scheme stored in public representations but also that which is cognitively present in the individual participant's mind) fulfills two functions from a theoretical point of view: it penetrates the action-representation system; it also (as we shall see later) activates a set of universal principles of religious ritual which assess the products generated by the system of rules in the action-representation system and in virtue of such an assessment constrain the conceptual scheme.

From a cognitivist perspective, the complex role of the conceptual scheme introduces a dynamic element into the system for the representation of religious ritual action. The psychological interest of the theory emerges at the point at which we attempt to ascertain the psychological reality of such an abstract description of the principles, processes, and products involved. In other words, how are the conceptual scheme, action-representation system, and universal principles (to be discussed next) related psychologically?

I think that the theses of the theory that McCauley and I have proposed are not only compatible with the cultural data in question; I also think that they are testable by the quite specific predictions that the theory makes about ritual participants' behavior, where such behavior consists of judgments uttered by ritual participants about ritual form.

The Universal Principles

Although a system for the representation of religious ritual action is a valuable heuristic device for locating cognitive patterns, especially when complemented by a conceptual scheme capable of providing the formal system with content, it achieves genuine theoretical significance when it is constrained by a set of universal principles. I now turn my attention to that feature of our theory of religious ritual action.

The action-representation system which we have described earlier is constrained by a set of universal principles. Following standard linguistic practice, we distinguish between substantive, formal, and functional universals (Lawson and McCauley 1990: 121–30). Substantive universals involve the categories and elements utilized in the rules; for example, participant, agent, action, object, quality, and so on. Formal universals have to do with the way the rules are organized, the order in which they are applied, and so on: for example, they might require that logically prior actions are also temporally prior.

Functional universals are the most significant for the purposes of our theory. Given our most fundamental assumption, namely the basic principle that all religious systems involve commitments to culturally postulated superhuman agents and that all religious ritual systems involve superhuman agents at some level of description (Lawson and McCauley 1990: 123–4), functional universals constrain the representation of ritual action. Two functional universal principles of religious ritual are the principle of superhuman agency and the principle of superhuman immediacy.

The principle of superhuman agency refers to the *character* of the superhuman agent's involvement in a ritual system as that involvement is specified in the structural description of a religious ritual. The significance of this principle of superhuman agency lies in its claim that where a superhuman agent functions as the *immediate* agent of an action upon an object of action, there we will find a ritual that is *central* to a religious system; for example, when Jesus as superhuman agent founds the church. However, where a superhuman agent is the *recipient* of action by another non-superhuman agent there we will find a more peripheral ritual; for example, when a ritual participant sacrifices a bowl of fruit to the appropriate superhuman agent. *What rituals are assumed to effect* (the terms of which will be provided by the conceptual scheme) depends crucially upon the action of superhuman agents—from the point of view of those with a mastery of the system.

The principle of superhuman immediacy involves not the character but the *immediacy* of the superhuman agent's involvement in a religious ritual's structural description. The *less* enabling actions that are required in order to implicate superhuman agency, the *more* fundamental the ritual; the more enabling actions that are required in order to implicate superhuman agency, the less fundamental the ritual will prove to be in the judgments that ritual participants make about the form and meaning of their rituals. The principle involves the notions of *ritual distance* and *ritual proximity;* for example, the act of a parishioner lighting a memorial candle requires more enabling actions than the pope installing a cardinal. An enabling action is any ritual action the prior performance of which is presupposed by the ritual under consideration.

I should add that *no particular* representation of superhuman agency in any ritual system is required, but *some representation or other* is a sine qua non for the motivation of religious ritual. I speak here of an identity of form but a variability of content.[4] Anyone can conceive of an agent with more abilities or different abilities than a human being possesses. Conceiving of a system that completely transcends the natural (and which does not mean "the artificial"!) is much more problematic. Whereas superhuman properties involve *matters of degree* (e.g., the ability to escape detection, the ability to overwhelm a powerful human being, and the ability to avoid disease), the term "supernatural" presupposes quite specific metaphysical commitments. You must first show what it means before you can employ it. McCauley and I have no interest in entering the metaphysical wars.

Consequences of the Theory

The theory of the representation of ritual action presented earlier has a number of consequences, some of them quite practical. Starting with the most practical, it need hardly be said that, equipped with such a theory of the representation of religious ritual action, a theory quite capable of delivering very precise descriptions of religious ritual structures (including those that are elaborately embedded), any anthropological field worker would be primed to ask new kinds of questions and seek new kinds of information from informants. Fieldworkers would be able to employ new formal techniques in the analysis of the materials they have gathered.

Such analyses promise interesting discoveries both about what structures are tacitly represented in the heads of the people in the culture studied, and, mutatis mutandis, what patterns of representation are distributed (see Sperber 1990) in the culture itself. Our theory underwrites the kinds of questions that will elicit judgments not only about what people know by tuition but also about what they know but do not realize they know, even though they have never been taught it. For example, the anthropologists will discover that ritual participants can be asked to make judgments not only about actual but also about possible rituals (theoretical rituals) and that their responses to these questions will disclose their ritual competence. The intuitions that participants will have about possible rituals will include the ability to sort out the imaginary but well formed and the imaginary but ill formed.

Our theory presents a way of describing the structures of competence underlying such judgments. An analysis of such structures promises to disclose novel relationships that will not easily be found by analyzing the conceptual scheme independently of its relationship to the action-representation system.

Other consequences of our theory include quite precise predictions about the judgments people are capable of making about ritual form (Lawson and McCauley 1990: 176). So, for example, our theory predicts (1) that ritual participants will distinguish religious ritual action from other kinds of religious action in conformity with the universal principles of the theory, (2) that ritual participants' judgments about the well-formedness of rituals and relative importance of a particular ritual to the ritual system as a whole will conform to the theory, (3) that ritual participants' judgments about the necessity of ritual repetition, the substitutability of agents and objects, and the reversibility or irreversibility of a ritual action will conform to the theory, and (4) that ritual participants' judgments about, and historical analyses of, religious systems' identities in times of alteration, transformation, or schism (i.e., in times of radical change) will be strongly correlated with our theory of ritual types.

These are hardly insignificant predictions. They ensure that the theory that we have proposed is independently testable, and they highlight the role that competence theorizing can play in dealing with cultural phenomena from a cognitivist perspective. They also raise the question of how such knowledge (understood now as tacit knowledge constraining particular judgments about particular ritual actions) was acquired. Few can seriously believe that such knowledge about well-formedness, repeatability, substitutability, reversibility, and so on is taught to members of a ritual in any thorough and explicit manner, if at all.

I am confident that cross-cultural studies of instruction and indoctrination will show, at most, that societies in their instructional situations will concentrate upon certain obvious principles taken seriously in the conceptual scheme prevalent in the society. Even when the contents of sequences of rituals *are* taught to initiates, little, if any, time will be spent *ranking* the centrality and importance of rituals. It will be enough to know what everybody is supposed to know about what to believe and what to do. More time will be spent on being sure that initiates get basic beliefs right, basic obligations ingrained. In any case, this is an empirical matter and can be tested in the field. I am reasonably sure that no time at all will be spent discussing either theoretical or possible rituals. The theoretical rituals (i.e., those in which superhuman agents appear in the structural description of the ritual as agents) will simply be assumed or stated as fact.

Clearly, people who are culturally competent will know how to cognitively manipulate ritual representations in such a manner that they are capable of issuing judgments about cultural form. The question is, then, how do they do so, if explicit cultural tuition is not available as an answer? Nativists will be inclined to look to biological structures, and cultural autonomists will be inclined to search for hidden cultural forces. Before we move in either direction, it is worthwhile considering what is at stake. Is it the case that such discrepancies between competence and tuition are either a biological or a cultural property? Not necessarily. First of all, it obviously is a *psychological* property. As I said at the very beginning of this chapter, it is a question of *what is acquired.* We are talking here about a form of knowledge, that is, the ability to make judgments about cultural form without explicit tuition. Now, what kind of psychological property is this form of knowledge? It is the kind of cognitive property which can be formally described by a system of rules capable of generating structural descriptions. So, given the semantic information provided by a conceptual scheme, all we need to acknowledge is that a system of rules and representations is capable of generating all the structural descriptions necessary for an explanation of the structure of the ritual system (as cognitively represented). So, the judgments about cultural form issued by the cultural participant (judgments which are independently testable by the predictions of the theory) can be deduced from the system of rules in relationship to a conceptual scheme and constrained by the universal principles.[5]

There are, then, two factors present. On the one hand, we have a set of interrelated abstract mechanisms (action-representation system, conceptual scheme, and universal principles) and an aggregation of cultural content which, *together,* are capable of accounting for the relevant properties of the phenomena in question. Obviously, however, such an argument does not account for the status of the abstract mechanisms. What are they abstractions from? One possible answer is that, given the fact that people are extraordinarily competent in recognizing certain kinds of patterns (and the structural descriptions of ritual action which our system generates are certainly patterns) and given the fact that artificial minds modeled along connectionist lines are capable of being trained up to recognize novel patterns on the basis of being presented with sets of examples, all we might need for an explanation of how a person is capable of making a judgment about well-formedness, or repeatability, and so on is to argue that our brains are so designed. In other words, our brains are excellent pattern-recognition devices. Pattern-recognition devices with a certain level of complexity in their internal structure (of a psychophysical kind and which may even include a rules-and-representation component) and trained by "experience" are quite capable of recognizing novel patterns with relative ease.

Such a connectionist view would not justify the view of a complete autonomous cultural system relentlessly transmitting information in a unidirectional manner to cultural participants. At most, it would show that human minds sufficiently trained over a long period of cognitive development in a cultural context are capable of recognizing novel patterns in cultural phenomena, and, in fact, are quite capable of contributing novel cognitive direction to prevailing cultural modes of behavior. That already would be a great leap forward in empirically accounting for cultural patterns.

But even if the connectionist picture does not sustain itself, a nativist view of such matters would in any case have to be cautious about deriving too much cultural content from innate form. Even in a principles-and-parameters approach to the acquisition of syntactic structures (Chomsky 1981), theoretical linguistics requires only that those universal principles that constrain all particular grammars be candidates for "innatehood." Much of the rest occurs at the psychological level and points to a level of complexity that needs to be acknowledged. In the same way, I am claiming that with a few mechanisms (a conceptual scheme, a set of action rules, and the universal principles) which represent a rich and complex set of cognitive processes, we can account for both the form and content of religious ritual. This is a level of theoretical description that is complex enough to engage our attention for some time to come.

Notes

1 In fact, recent research (Pettito and Marentette 1991) seems to confirm nativist views about universal linguistic constraints by showing that deaf children commence the first stages of the acquisition of language, in this

FORMS AND STRUCTURES 53

case sign language, by the age of ten months, despite not being exposed to speech. Interestingly, though, visual cues appear to be capable of acting as substitutes for phonological parameters.

2 In this chapter, I do not employ the formalism that McCauley and I propose in *Rethinking Religion*. Instead, I use a qualitative description of the theory of the representation of ritual action and present some of its results.

3 Dealing with the role played by objects in religious conceptual schemes is complicated. Internal to the description of the structure of a ritual action, the object agency filter is crucial; but it is not the only resource available in religious systems for handling problematic objects. For example, when analyzing the relationships among a set of ritual actions, situations occur in which objects are ritually transformed ("this bread, on this plate . . . ") into agents, which then in subsequent rituals can act as agents.

4 The term "superhuman" is preferable to the term "supernatural," as a property that ritual agents must either have or presuppose, because whereas the term "superhuman" requires no ontological commitment about the superhuman agent on the part of the theorist, the term "supernatural" certainly does.

5 In my view, there is no need to assume that a culture is one system, with different aspects, all of which have an underlying unity. A culture may be nothing more than a set of cognitively generated systems which affect each other without being thoroughly integrated into an overarching cultural unity. A culture might very well be more like a second-rate orchestra without a conductor trying to play a vaguely remembered tune. Of course, this fact about culture may also be a picture of what the mind is like.

References

Boyer, Pascal (1990). *Tradition as Truth and Communication*, Cambridge: Cambridge University Press.

Laura-Ann Pettito, and Paul F. Marentette (1991). "Babbling in the ManualMode: Evidence for the Ontogeny of Language," *Science* 251 (5000): 1493–6.

Lawson E. Thomas, and Robert N. McCauley (1990). *Rethinking Religion: Connection Cognkition and Culture*, Cambridge: Cambridge University Press.

INTRODUCTION TO CHAPTER 5

The concept of evoked culture has fascinated me ever since I read about it in the work of Tooby and Cosmides. It takes the concept of capacity or disposition very seriously and employs the notion of calibration by environmental factors as a key to explaining cultural variation. While such variation is real, it is never the complete story about human nature and, in fact, recovers the very notion all too often lost in cultural relativism.

5

Evoked and Transmitted Culture

The notion of culture has long been a bone of contention in the social sciences, particularly in cultural anthropology. Issues about its ontological status, its causal properties, have been the grist for the philosophical mill for a long time. Philosophers of science have shown an interest in analyzing the role the concept plays in the social sciences and have particularly focused on its relationship to biology in general and to evolutionary theory in particular.

Everyone interested in the subject of the relation between cognition and culture is aware that if you travel from Cape Town to Cairo, you will encounter many different social arrangements, many different languages, many different modes of thought, many different foods, and many different modes of dress. In fact, such a trip will expose you to cultural diversity, that diversity will consist of ideas, practices, and the effects such ideas and practices have on the conditions people within which live their lives. Cultural relativists insist that that is the bottom line. Don't bother to search for universals because variation is all there is. Strictly speaking there is no such thing as human nature. Ironically, such scholars are also deterministic because if there are no generalizations across human populations, then any ideas and practices in that population determine

EVOKED AND TRANSMITTED CULTURE

how you think and what you do and how you arrange your life. The pattern of your life is determined by the surrounding cultural facts.

This idea is not crazy because as you move north from the Cape you will find it somewhat difficult to fit into a new social arrangement, and an incomprehensible language, sometimes radically different foods, different social hierarchies, and so on. But there are two concepts that help us to explain and thereafter understand such puzzlements, "evoked culture" and "transmitted culture." Evoked culture focuses on evolved human capacities and how environmental capacities shape and calibrate those capacities. Language is a good example. There is little question that the capacity to acquire a language is universal, and that natural selection designed our brains so that at a certain point humans became capable of both inventing and responding to linguistic cues, The fact that the cues differed in novel environments accounts for the diversity of languages.

So, we account for diversity by certain cultural cues and we account for the development of a particular language being developed at all by cultural cues. Different patterns emerge in different environmental conditions

There is another mechanism at work as well, that transmits information from one mind to another, the notion of transmitted cultural information. The best account of this process is the epidemiology of representations suggested by Dan Sperber (1985) who proposes both an individual and a population account of the transmission process. The individual account describes the process from one mind to another where the information is not copied but reconstructed. So even though the process requires the capacity to receive the information it does not determine the accurate reception of that information. It really is a process of reconstructing the information and where a faithful copying is only the limiting case,

The population account employs the notion of attractor. A set of reconstructed, transmitted information in a cultural situation will converge on a relatively stable concept that makes communication not only possible but interesting and also ultimately enables us to cross boundaries, try new foods, appreciate cultural differences and even learn new languages. The younger we are the more capable we are of doing so.

When I began taking an interest in psychology behavioral psychology under the influence of B.F. Skinner was the standard approach to accounting for human behavior and thought. Any form of behavior could be accounted for by environmental variables according to the official doctrine. In the social sciences socialization provided the complete causal story. In psychology mind was absent and in the social sciences largely ignored, partly because of the notion of the autonomy of the social fact. At the same time cultural anthropology was deep into cultural relativism and was not at all interested in engaging in a conversation with either evolutionary biology or psychology, opting instead for interpretive exclusivism. Of course, the cognitive revolution changed all of that.

An important moment occurred in the rise of a new linguistics. The linguistic revolution argued that all humans were equipped with a language acquisition device. Some psychologists, aware of the limits of radical behaviorism began to take notice of evolutionary biology, and some anthropologists began to talk to those psychologists who were talking to biologists and eventually began to talk to each other, meanwhile inviting philosophers of mind and philosophers of science to join the conversation. Exciting times. In fact, cognitive science became an interdisciplinary conversation among scientifically minded people from many disciplines. A great deal of theoretical research and experimentation eventually got underway to test the claims made by these cognitive scientists. The study of infants in particular blossomed because the notion of human dispositions or capacities was crucial for understanding cognitive development. There were many surprises.

Early discussions revolved around issues of nature versus nurture and what was innate and what was not, one thing became apparent and that was that humans were not born with minds which were not blank slates. Slowly the research became more sophisticated as theory and experiment made advances. Now that the mind was back in play we could propose and study mental mechanisms employing many different methods supported by novel theories. And not only that, we could place the history of the mind in evolutionary perspective.

The subject of how we learn what we learn is now studied in many ways. Some scientists study the process by focusing on infant development, others in animal studies, some of it comparative between humans and specific kinds of animals. Some scientists employ the methods available in artificial intelligence. Others study human communication and model the interchange of information and what capacities, conditions and environmental variables are thought to be at work. In the work that Robert N McCauley and I have done we have focused upon notions such as ritual form and suggested both universal principles and contextual factors at work.

We still have a long way to go as we explore these human capacities. Whatever claims we make, for example if we argue that there are circuits in the brain designed by the process of natural selection we had better be able to predict deficits in human behavior because mechanisms of any kind always run into problems. In any case, I think that the concepts of evoked and transmitted culture is here to stay.

References

Sperber, Dan (1985). "Anthropology and Psychology: Towards an Epidemiology of Representations," *Man* 20: 73–89.

PART II

Cognition and the Imagination

INTRODUCTION TO CHAPTER 6

I have been an avid reader of science fiction for many years. The study of religion is replete with imaginary beings. Some of the time, science fiction authors find their characters in religious narratives little realizing that the reason these out of this world characters tap the same psychological roots as their religious counterparts.

6

Cognitive Constraints on Imagining Other Worlds

Every science fiction reader gravitates toward a favorite set of authors. I find myself returning toward the same spot on the bookstore's shelves where I hope to find the next book published by one of my favorites; I typically check to see whether Nancy Kress has recently published a new book. When I discover that she has, I often make something of a fool of myself in the quiet aisles of the bookstore by saying rather loudly, "Yes!!" I was particularly enthralled by Kress's Probability Trilogy and have read it a number of times.

The three interlinked stories *Probability Moon, Probability Sun,* and *Probability Space* involve the expansion of humankind into the far reaches of the galaxy, where they have encountered the Fallers, who not only will not communicate with them but also are bent on their destruction. In fact, the Fallers are xenophobic. Much of the narrative hinges on whether the people of the Earth can find the means to defeat or isolate the Fallers. Humankind has also discovered a new planet populated by sentient creatures who operate according to "shared reality." Shared reality involves living according to a set of norms for the conduct of life that, if flouted, causes head pain to the transgressors. It is a physiological condition. Shared reality proves a powerful technique for maintaining a stable and productive society but also creates problems for the strangers from Earth, who do not have this condition.

In orbit around this newly discovered planet is an extremely powerful object that contains settings on an incremental scale that, when triggered, can wreak havoc not only on entire planetary systems but also seems to be capable at its highest setting of disrupting the fabric of space-time itself. A similar object lies deeply buried on the planet and is responsible, through the processes of evolution, for the "shared reality" behavior of the sentient creatures on the planet. To permit either the orbiting object or the buried object to fall into the hands of the Fallers would tip the balance in favor of those destroyers. To remove the object hidden underneath the surface of the planet would, moreover, destroy "shared reality" for the inhabitants; it would, however, provide a powerful weapon in the battle with the Fallers. It is very important, therefore, that the people of Earth get their hands on this weapon first. Kress characterizes both the Fallers and the inhabitants of the planet deftly and with an imaginative flourish and at the same time raises powerful moral issues about doing harm to alien cultures. A trilogy of this kind is capable of grabbing the reader's attention.

I found the characters of the *Probability Trilogy* persuasively described, its science intriguing, and its moral tone provocative. Reading this trilogy led me to reflect on the obviously complex creative processes that an author mines in order to weave a story of such mind-bending imagination. As a cognitive scientist interested in the creative process, reading this trilogy made me wonder what is involved in imagining other worlds and other creatures such as those that populate the pages of this fascinating story. And because of the science involved, the trilogy also persuaded me to pursue the question of whether reading science fiction is an aid or a hindrance to developing a deeper understanding of scientific knowledge.

Here I will focus on both of these issues. I will discuss the processes that lead to novel ideas such as those found in Kress's work. I will also pay attention to the role that science fiction can play in leading the reader to a deeper knowledge of science.

Certainly, the creativity involved in imagining and writing such a story comes from a great deal of hard work rather than precipitously from some transcendent, illuminating vision. Of course, there sometimes comes the puzzling dream rich with meaning, the moment of illumination that makes connections not recognized before, the penny dropping that rings the cognitive bells. However, the fertile soil has long been prepared by the grind. None of the authors that I know are lazy. They might have periods when they stare endlessly at the blank page hoping for some special moment that will force their fingers to make some intelligible marks on the page. Typically, however, these moments seldom come and writers soon realize that they had better get on with the job. Actually, the same goes for scientific theorizing, which, hopefully, will lead to experiments that will either confirm or disconfirm the hypotheses under consideration.

Whether we are dealing with the making of imaginative literature or the pursuit of scientific inquiry, a great deal of background knowledge is essential before we can even hope to solve the problems that present themselves to us in either of these modes of creativity. What I wish to accomplish here, therefore, is not to explain what creativity is or even how it arises; authors such as Mihaly Csikszentmihalyi (1996) have written outstanding works on the subject. Rather, as a cognitive scientist deeply involved in searching for clues about the workings of the human mind, especially as these workings give rise to the products of the imagination, my goal is to identify and discuss whether there are any constraints on creativity and what might be required for their beneficial use. Of particular interest to me are the strategies that might lead to novel ideas, especially those found in works of science fiction.

Now, one commonsense notion about creative activity assumes that we all possess the mental equipment to imagine anything. Most commonsense notions contain a grain of truth and sometimes bushels of it. We shall see later, however, that common sense, while useful and relevant in many situations, does have its limitations. Dealing with this problem becomes particularly interesting when we examine works of imaginative literature, particularly those forms that involve the invention of other worlds and the beings that populate them, the worlds imagined by the authors of science fiction.

To uncover some of the secrets of the creative imagination means looking to the mind for answers. Cognitive scientists have taken as their job the task of figuring out how the mind works. They attempt to answer the question of what the various levels of cognitive processing are. Simply put, cognition is how we come to know the world and cognitive science involves theorizing about the various processes that produce such knowledge. One technique employed in achieving the goal of defining the architecture of the mind involves starting with the notion of *constraint* and analyzing how this feature might apply to our understanding of the workings of the mind.

To view the human mind as operating under constraints is to recognize two important factors. The first of these is the notion of limitation, or, if you prefer, restriction. To speak of a limitation is not to make claims about what the mind cannot do; rather it means understanding the conditions that characterize the mind's work. For example, working (or short-term) memory operates under severe limitations. Remembering more than seven or eight chunks of information after just one exposure (such as a string of numbers) is very difficult for the vast majority of people. Mnemonic savants are few and far between. Long-term memory, on the other hand, can be triggered in amazingly complex and interesting ways. Vivid recall of long-gone events under special conditions occurs to all of us. A smell can evoke your memory of an event that occurred many years ago. So, a limitation does not mean a prohibition. Obviously, we do remember some things for a brief moment in time and others for long periods. That simply means that there are different conditions for short- and long-term memory.

In fact, knowing that the mind operates according to limitations leads us to recognize that constraints are also enabling devices. They make the development of certain forms of knowledge possible. On the basis of a simple mechanism such as a set of concepts like the number "one" and the notion of "successor," we can produce an infinite number of mathematical operations. The discipline of linguistics has been able to show that a finite set of rules can produce an infinite number of sentences. And of course, we all know about the butterfly effect, which shows how easy it is to destabilize a system in equilibrium.

The moral of all of this is that our minds work as well as they do because of the constraints under which they operate, whether these involve working or long-term memory or the processes that lead to the creation of novel ideas. These constraints channel and direct the way we reason about the world. Imagining new worlds is, after all, a form of reasoning about what is possible. Evolutionary psychologists, who look both to evolutionary biology and to cognitive science in their attempts to explain the regularities in human thought and behavior (despite the obvious differences in cultural practices that the thoughts inform), argue that the various functions that our minds evince are the products of natural selection. The constraints according to which our minds operate have emerged as properties of the human brain because they have adaptive value. Sometimes it is as simple as the capacity to plan, to think ahead. On the ancestral plains, planning where you will be when the animals come around the hill can mean the difference between starvation and plenty. Sometimes these processes are much more complicated, as when we try to figure out complex social relationships such as "I know that Jane thinks that Jack despises his brother Joe because he rather than Jack would love to surprise his mother with a present even though it is not her birthday."

Cognitive science, aided and abetted by evolutionary, cognitive, and developmental psychology, hypothesizes that we are designed by the forces of natural selection to operate in terms of a folk physics, a folk biology, and a folk psychology as our basic ways of trafficking with the world. Folk physics is a commonsense "theory" of what the material world is like according to such notions as solidity, dimensionality, continuity, and so forth. Folk biology, likewise, is a commonsense theory of what the organic world is like according to such notions as birth, reproduction, growth, development, and death. Folk psychology is a commonsense theory that attributes desires, beliefs, hopes, wishes, fears, and so on to humans and even some animals. Each of these intuitive systems of knowledge, which operate under the constraints that come with such design, enables us to survive and reproduce our kind precisely because they are such useful forms of knowledge for living in and manipulating our environment.

These intuitive forms of knowledge also seem to place restrictions on our imagination including the creative thinking involved in the production of science fiction. Each form of folk knowledge consists in a system that is responsive to particular domains of experience: the material world, the organic world, and the world of intentionality. Each form of knowledge operates according to a certain set of constraints that both limit and enable our perceptions and conceptions of our environment and ourselves.

How do we know this and what can we do about it? Let us turn, therefore, to some scientific work to focus on the role that constraints play as both limiting and enabling devices when we imagine other worlds and the creatures that the authors so cleverly persuade us inhabit them. Thomas B. Ward (1995) and his colleagues have been in the vanguard of the study of creative idea generation. For more than a decade he has steadily advanced our knowledge of how human beings creatively produce novel notions. His model of investigation involves what he has called "the path of least resistance" (1994). He says: "When people develop new ideas for a particular domain, the predominant tendency is to retrieve fairly specific, basic level exemplars from that domain, select one or more of those retrieved instances as a starting point, and project many of the stored properties of the instances onto the novel ideas being developed" (Ward 1994: 3). For example, Ward has shown that when participants in an experimental study were asked to imagine animals on other planets, 90 percent of the properties of these imaginary animals possessed the same properties as those of Earth animals; they possessed eyes, legs, and bilateral symmetry. Ward reports that even when his subjects were instructed to make their imaginary creatures radically different, the results were nevertheless largely the same (1997). What seems to be at work here is that our intuitive knowledge is a powerful force in divining what might be out there according to the domains that each folk theory is particularly responsive to.

Ward's goal in the experiments that he and his colleagues have devised is to identify the various strategies that lead to differing degrees of novelty as well as to uncover the potential for improving creative functioning (2004: 1). This goal is particularly important for understanding why some science fiction writers are so successful in persuading us of the verisimilitude of their novels. It seems that while some science fiction writers follow the path of least resistance by simply extending the properties of creatures that they know to other creatures, some authors seem capable of imagining other the inhabitants of other worlds in such interesting and creative ways that they capture and rivet our attention. While the path of least resistance delivers the familiar idea, to learn how to overcome this path promises greater excitement, insight, and knowledge.

From a scientific point of view, the work done by Ward and his colleagues has provided important clues about the strategies that are employed in imagining worlds beyond our own. According to Ward, some experimental subjects typically employ the imaginative strategy of dreaming up creatures based on specific, earthbound animals that they are acquainted with. They utilize an *exemplar strategy*. Others employ an alternative strategy by reasoning more *abstractly*. That is to say, they take into consideration abstract principles such as the environmental characteristics that might be the case on other planets and then imagine what the properties of the creatures would most probably have to be to exist in that alien environment. Operating according to abstract rather than specific constraints does not, of course, eliminate cognitive constraints; the point is rather that there are different constraints that not only limit our imaginative products but also enable our imaginations to flower in more interesting and compelling ways. For example, to know something about the laws of nature that characterize the physical world does not mean that one has escaped from the tendencies of the human mind to follow the path of least resistance. Reflective thought, which is also a property of human minds, is able to take the reasoning process as its object of attention. This means that our minds are able to operate at levels of abstraction (when appropriately trained). There appear to be constraints at this level of mental operation as well, but it is here that notions such as systematicity, coherence, evidence, logic, and so forth provide the constraints.

The experiments involved in establishing the fact of constraints are interesting in their own right. One group of subjects (the abstract condition) was asked to imagine the fundamental properties of animals generally and then to consider how these properties would be expressed on another world quite different from our own. This group was told that they should not use Earth animals as examples, but instead should think of principles such as what it would take to survive in an alien environment quite different from the Earth's. Another group (the exemplar condition) was encouraged to think of specific Earth animals and then imagine what these animals would have to be like on another world. The third group (the control condition) was simply told to imagine animals on another world. According to the analysis of the data by independent coders of the results of the experiment, the subjects operating in the abstract condition clearly produced the most creative ideas.

In another experiment Ward and his colleagues (2004) had all of the subjects imagine, draw, and describe a living thing that might exist on another planet. Some of the participants in the experiment were given exemplar instructions, others were given abstract principles, and the control group was given no special instructions other than to imagine a living thing on another planet. The differences in what the participants imagined were significant. Those who employed the abstract strategy produced far more interesting and intriguing notions than either the exemplar or the control group.

What can we learn from these experiments? First, there is a tendency to use the path of least resistance when imagining novel situations unless one is encouraged to employ a more fruitful strategy. Second, thinking harder (i.e., thinking more abstractly) pays dividends when solving problems and imagining novel entities and situations. Third, writing an interesting science fiction novel that will stretch the mind of the reader involves not only expecting the reader to think more abstractly but also having the author employ the cognitive strategy that will capture the interest of the reader and will lead to a deeper understanding of the science in the science fiction. Employing this strategy involves the author accessing systematic principles that appeal to notions such as evidence, deduction, induction, and so forth rather than simply extending a tried-and-true idea to new instances, for example, moving the nostrils to below the mouth when describing an alien creature.

The third point requires elaboration because it most probably goes beyond what the experiments have shown. Before I engage in that elaboration, however, I wish to make one point, namely, that the best science fiction writers do not usually follow the path of least resistance. Instead, they build entirely new worlds on the basis of the scientific knowledge that they have accumulated. As with most scientific knowledge, it is not only systematic, well-defined, and mathematically based; rather, one of the most interesting features of scientific knowledge is that it goes against the expectations that follow from our typical use of folk theories in our reasoning about the world. Such scientific knowledge is counterintuitive. In other words, it contravenes our intuitions of what the physical, the biological, and the mental worlds are like.

Science fiction writers understand the counterintuitiveness of scientific knowledge and, therefore, recognize the need to build a novel world on the basis of scientific knowledge. Science fiction writers, at least the good ones, having done their world building, then, are ready to imagine the types of creatures that would have to fit into the alien conditions provided by their novel worlds, populated by creatures who have to survive hazardous conditions such as intense radiation or deal with relativistic effects in traveling astronomical distances.

Neither our folk physics nor our folk biology nor our folk psychology prepares us for understanding the counterintuitive concepts that populate scientific theories and the stories those theories have inspired. It is important, therefore, for science fiction authors to devise a means in their storytelling for persuading us that the arcane notions of, for example,

66   IMAGINING THE COGNITIVE SCIENCE OF RELIGION

quantum mechanics, natural selection, and the unconscious processes that lie beneath our conscious reflections make sense. This does not mean that the task of scientific education lies with science fiction novelists alone. Some of the great scientists have also been great communicators of scientific knowledge. A few, such as Gregory Benford, have also been science fiction writers.

When I think of great scientists who have wrestled with the counterintuitive nature of scientific theory, I am reminded of the ability of Richard Feynman to convey both the excitement and the puzzling features of physics. I will never forget working through *Six Easy Pieces* (Feynman 1995) and finally arriving at Chapter 6, "Quantum Behavior." The counterintuitive nature of this area of physics is obvious. Feynman says there:

> Quantum mechanics is the description of the behavior of matter in all its details and, in particular, of the happenings on an atomic scale. Things on a very small scale behave like nothing that you have any direct experience about. They do not behave like waves, they do not behave like particles, they do not behave like clouds or billiard balls or weights on springs, or like anything else you have seen. (116)

In other words, we have no exemplars from the ordinary world of our experience that allow us to imagine what is going on at the level of quantum mechanics. What, then, does it take to comprehend the discoveries of quantum behavior? It certainly takes the ability to engage in abstract thought rather than the path of least resistance. Perhaps even more important, it takes a special language, the language of mathematics, to express formally what we cannot conceive of imagistically. We can, of course, imagine thought experiments that will show what is going on at this level. In fact, that is what Feynman does in order to introduce us to quantum behavior. But do we really understand what is going on? Only if by "understand" we mean the ability to express the ideas involved in quantum mechanics in a language that describes the processes involved, the language of mathematics.

It is not only at the level of the very small that such problems of understanding arise, however. Finding the reality beneath appearances occurs at all levels of scientific inquiry. For example, psychologists have been able to show that people are typically essentialists in their thinking about the biological world. Essentialism is the view that a member of any category, such as dog, human, or tree, possesses a property that determines its identity. We all know, for example, that giraffes are quite different from elephants, frogs, and trees. All of us, some of the time, think in essentialist terms. Certainly, we would be most upset if we mistook a tree for a frog! But from an evolutionary point of view (the long view), elephants, trees, and frogs have a common origin *if you*

OTHER WORLDS

go back far enough and have the right theory. But the long view is not all that helpful in our day-to-day traffic with the world—unless a situation arises that requires a scientific explanation of why, for instance, the pollen from a bush might cause an allergic reaction in someone.

From a psychological point of view, it makes sense to notice these differences between the organisms that inhabit the Earth. Precisely because the short view is so useful, it serves as a hindrance to accepting that there are hidden mechanisms at work that can explain why organisms differ from each other. The resistance to Darwin and the neo-Darwinian synthesis is still very strong. I have been impressed with the frequency with which science fiction authors in all kinds of subtle ways introduce ideas of natural selection in their explanations of why a certain type of alien creature possesses the properties that it does.

Only when we arrive at the psychological level of analysis, however, does resistance to scientific explanations of human behavior raise its ugly head in a particularly virulent form. Fundamentalists may complain about the evils of the "theory" of evolution—at worst insisting upon the truth of creationist mythology, and at best arguing for intelligent design—but when it comes to explaining why humans behave in the way that they do, why people tend to do one thing rather than another, and when psychologists appeal to hidden cognitive mechanisms that account for observable fact, then a chorus of dissent arises from some scholars in the humanities, especially those with postmodernist commitments. Then charges of "scientism" abound, and we are told it is not nature but nurture, as if any knowledgeable scientist would deny that with respect to the organic world nature and nurture were inextricably intertwined.

While resistance to scientific knowledge has a certain cachet, unless such knowledge conveniently serves ideological purposes, scientific knowledge proves particularly problematic when it fails to match our normal intuitions or expectations about what the world is like. But there is an irony here because it is also the case that people respond to counterintuitive ideas because they capture our attention. Developmental psychologists have shown that infants pay attention and act surprised when counterintuitive events are brought to their attention. In fact, cognitive scientists who have analyzed the process of cultural transmission have argued that counterintuitive ideas (such as mythological narratives) have a transmission advantage if the violations to intuitive expectations are minimal. If the violations are too great, then we lose interest because we know that is not the way the world is. This obviously creates a problem for scientific explanations because, as we have seen in the case of quantum behavior, nothing *in our experience* prepares us for the anomalous fact that scientific theorizing discloses. Both scientists and science fiction writers, therefore, are faced with a problem how to communicate novel and puzzling and sometimes outrageous ideas. In the case of science, the program is clear years of training in the particular science, whether it be physics, chemistry, biology, or psychology. That means acquiring all of the tools, concepts, and experimental procedures necessary to discover new knowledge.

Science fiction writers have a different problem. They need both to understand the science they will employ in their fiction and also to successfully convince even scientifically naïve readers that the worlds that they imagine are possible worlds. The easy way out would be to follow the path of least resistance, but this would be at the expense of more creative results as experimental work has shown.

Nancy Kress seldom follows the path of least resistance. Take the notion of "shared reality" that Kress has imagined. Given the kinds of brains that we have and given the most plausible theories about how those brains enable us to reason about the world, human beings typically construct their view of what is real based on cues from the environment, such cues triggering cognitive mechanisms designed by evolution to respond to the cues in the various domains. We build our knowledge of the real, whether this be physical, biological, or psychological, by interacting with our environment using the competencies with which the processes of natural selection have endowed us. Certainly, some of that knowledge comes about by explicit instruction, but even that kind of knowledge makes sense to us because we already have the equipment, the cognitive resources, to appropriate the information conveyed to us by formal and informal education.

What Kress has imagined is a mind similar to ours in many respects but which, because of special conditions of a physical kind, is particularly responsive to violations of cultural norms. To contravene these norms means that the contraveners are "not real" and therefore not worthy of being communicated with or cooperated with. In fact, they are a threat to those who live in a world of "shared reality." Of course, an author must be careful because the reader typically will tend to follow the path of least resistance, so elements of the story will have to connect with the typical constraints that characterize our way of acquiring knowledge. Not everything can be novel because then the story will lose its interest. So there had better also be romantic relationships, situations of conflict, desires, and goals that appeal effortlessly to us when we follow the path of least resistance.

Another example of Kress's ability to imagine other worlds according to abstract principles is her idea of "space tunnels" through which individuals safely ensconced in a spaceship can almost instantaneously move from one place in the galaxy to another. Here Kress employs the idea of quantum entanglement, an idea that is completely counterintuitive to our folk physics. She extends this idea to the notion of macrolevel object entanglement. She clues the reader into the fact that physicists have developed the notion of quantum entanglement which she then defines for the reader as the possibility that one particle affects its paired counterpart regardless of distance. I can imagine an adventurous teacher in an introductory physics class recommending that the student read the probability trilogy not only for fun but also for profit and then raising the question of whether macrolevel object entanglement is either possible or prohibited by the laws of physics. Some budding particle physicists in the classroom might be inspired to make new discoveries about the hidden world that hides beneath appearances.

Or take the idea of the attitude of the Fallers to other forms of life besides their own. Is it possible for a society to survive when it demonstrates such an extreme hostility? That is an interesting question. Certainly, there are sufficient examples from the peoples of the Earth to recognize the presence of xenophobia in many human societies. The sad truth is that human beings are particularly susceptible to basing their decisions about other ways of life on superficial characteristics. Clannishness is always with us, and racism has been very difficult to eliminate even in democratic societies. If we wish to follow the path of least resistance, even though this is in many ways a useful approach, we shall miss the opportunity to develop those aspects of our mind that can lead to ever more insightful concepts about the world in which we live. Science fiction writers, because of their commitment to scientific discoveries, contribute to the development of the growth of our knowledge.

References

Csikszentmihalyi, Mihaly (1996). *Creativity: Flow and the Psychology of Discovery and Invention*, New York: HarperCollins.

Feynman, Richard P. (1995). *Six Easy Pieces: Essentials of Physics Explained by Its Most Brilliant Teacher*, Reading: Addison-Wesley Publishing Company.

Ward, Thomas B. (1994). "Structured Imagination: The Role of Conceptual Structure in Exemplar Generation," *Cognitive Psychology* 27: 1–40.

Ward, Thomas B. (1995). "What's Old about New Ideas?" in *The Creative Cognition Approach*, edited by S. M. Smith, T. B. Ward, and R. A. Finke, 157–78, Cambridge, MA: MIT Press.

Ward, Thomas B., and C. M. Sifonis (1997). "Task Demands and Generative Thinking: What Changes and What Remains the Same?" *Journal of Creative Behavior* 31: 245–59.

Ward, Thomas B., Merryl J. Patterson, and C. M. Sifonis (2004). "The Role of Specificity and Abstraction in Creative Idea Generation," *Creativity Research Journal* 16: 1–9.

INTRODUCTION TO CHAPTER 7

Today when we call something a myth, we mean an engaging, fascinating but obviously false story, but many scholars in the humanities and social sciences are not so quick to rush to judgment. Not to argue that they are true but that their importance lies at a different level of analysis. I point to the importance of Claude Levi-Strauss in being an early figure in identifying the cognitive features of myth. In his engaging books he was most interested in showing us how an examination of myth gave us clues about how the human mind works. Those captivating stories handed down from generation to generation capture our attention for a reason even when we know that they are false.

7

The Explanation of Myth and Myth as Explanation

A long tradition exists for identifying myth as a species of explanation. After suffering a period of eclipse by what I shall call the tradition of deflection, it has emerged with a new brilliance and has provoked discussion in both the social sciences and the humanities. The purpose of this chapter is to critically evaluate aspects of the new explanatory tradition and to show that the structuralist approach developed by Claude Levi-Strauss, which has connections with this reemergent tradition, advances our knowledge of the nature of myth.

The general position of the explanatory tradition in its earlier phase has been characterized variously as rationalistic, intellectualistic, or cognitivist. An often-forgotten version of the intellectualist position is that myths are to be thought of as literal and right explanations of the world. I suppose that Bishop

EXPLANATION OF MYTH, MYTH AS EXPLANATION

Usher's dating of the creation of the world at 4004 BC would be an example of this version. A theory not so easily forgotten is that myths were literal but wrong explanations of the world. Sir James Frazer, for example, wrote that myths were mistaken explanations of phenomena, whether of human life or of external nature (Fontenrose 1971: 1).

An initial response to, partial reaction against, but not total rejection of, this earlier intellectualist interpretation of myth occurred within the shifting boundaries of the symbolist movement. Even when the identification of myths as explanations appeared to be completely rejected by the symbolists, an interest remained in relating myths to cognitive processes of however vaguely defined a character. Quite frequently a theory of representation replaced a theory of explanation. Or else myths became identified with an autonomous form of the human spirit (Bidney 1965: 8).

The tradition of myth as an instance of explanation, whether or not it includes the symbolist movement, was deflected, but certainly not destroyed, by a number of theories and methods of inquiry developed in the earlier part of the twentieth century. I have reference to functionalism, *Verstehen* methodology (Abel 1948), and what has been called the "linguistic turn" in philosophy. These three approaches depended, respectively, on the work of Malinowski (1948) and Radcliffe-Brown, Dilthey and Weber, and Wittgenstein (in his later period). This tradition of deflection mounted a massive critique of earlier methods of inquiry into, and theories about, human life and thought and, in fact, directed stringent criticism against the prevailing modes and logics of scientific inquiry itself.

From time to time in this revolution attention was paid to myths, for, as has often been the case in the course of the intellectual history of Western culture, myths seemed an eminently useful cultural artifact for illustrating certain very important problems about the nature of human thought. When such attention was paid, there was an insistence upon rejecting or severely qualifying the theory of myths as explanations of "human life or of external nature," to use Frazer's phrase. In the tradition of deflection, even the symbolist view came under attack. (This is not surprising because, as John Skorupski [1976] has shown, the symbolist movement depends upon the intellectualist tradition.) Malinowski (1948) asserted, for example, that "studied alive, myth, as we shall see, is not symbolic, but a direct expression of its subject matter; it is not an explanation in satisfaction of a scientific interest, but a narrative resurrection of a primeval reality, told in satisfaction of deep religious wants, moral cravings, social submissions, assertions, even practical requirements" (100). In his approach to myth and ritual, magic and religion, Malinowski (1948) rejects both the intellectualist and the symbolic interpretation of myths. Instead, he suggests paying attention to the psychological and social *functions* of myth. As a consequence, a new method and theory of human life and thought is finally made explicit. It was named functionalism.

Richard Rudner (1966) has called this tradition of deflection, as it finds expression in the social sciences, the separatist position (84), and of it, May Brodbeck (1968) has said: "There are clearly two factions within the social disciplines. One of them exuberantly embraces the scientific ideal: the other exalts its own intuitive understanding as being superior in logic and in principle to scientific explanation of the ways of man" (2). In this separatist tradition of intuitive understanding in the social sciences, as well as in humanistic studies, much has been made of the distinction between *Verstehen* and explanation, and historians of religion and philosophers of religion have not given the position an unfavorable reception. Anyone interested in the study of religion in general or myth and ritual, in particular, will recognize the slogans which have emerged from the movement: "look for the intention," "examine the consequences," "find the use," and "what are its effects?"

A significant critique of the logical and methodological issues involved in the tradition of deflection exists (Penner 1971, Hempel 1968) and will not be repeated here. This critique has been so powerful and penetrating that any scholar of religion ignores it at his intellectual peril. Business cannot continue as usual; it certainly has not in much of the social sciences and the humanities.

A New Approach

The bankruptcy of the tradition of deflection (which is not dead by any means) is one important reason for the reemergence of the explanatory tradition. Past mistakes, insistently pointed to by the tradition of deflection, have been instructive. For example, scholars in this new intellectualist tradition have learned that context and function cannot be ignored even if they do not provide causal explanations of human life and thought, that all knowledge is theory dependent, that use and function are heuristically important, and that translation from one language to another and comparisons between cultures are by no means unambiguous operations and involve logical as well as empirical issues. But what is of interest here is that the new intellectualist tradition has recovered a concern for explanation. In the process it has also argued that *myths are a kind of explanation.* The problem has been what the *status* of such putative mythic explanations is.

Four versions of this new explanatory theory may be identified: the theory of formal continuity but idiomatic discontinuity, the theory of conceptual relativism, the theory of rational dualism, and the theory of situational logic.

The Theory of Formal Continuity but Idiomatic Discontinuity between Myth as Explanation and Science as Explanation

One of the most ingenious and influential attempts at recovering the earlier theory of myths as "explanations of phenomena whether of human life or of external nature" without simply repeating the views of the earlier intellectualist tradition is the theory of the social anthropologist Robin Horton. He argues that traditional religious thought (of which myths would be one expression) has a formal identity with scientific thought. This equivalence (his own term) between these two modes of thought is characterized by an interest in theoretical explanation specifiable in eight ways. Whatever differences are discoverable between religious and scientific thought may be attributed to a *difference in idiom* and is traceable to the character of the social systems in which they respectively occur. According to Horton, societies in which science is predominant have a special attitude of openness. Societies in which religion is predominant have a special attitude of closedness. In open societies the idiom for the expression of theoretical explanations of the world is impersonal. In closed societies the idiom is personal. But while the conceptual functions of both types of explanation are equivalent, Horton also wishes to side with science. He says:

> All this is not to deny that science has progressed greatly through working in a non-personal theoretical idiom. I am inclined to believe that it is this idiom, and this idiom only, which will eventually lead to the triumph of science in human affairs. . . . For the progressive acquisition of knowledge man needs both the right kind of theories and the right attitude toward them. But it is only the latter which we call science. (153)

What makes science right and traditional thought wrong, according to Horton, is that in traditional cultures there is no developed awareness of alternatives to the established body of theoretical tenets (153). Being unable to imagine possible alternatives to such theories, the religious thinker employs what Horton calls the *"ad hoc* technique of secondary elaboration,"* that is, the search for rationalizations to explain the failures of the theories.

Horton's theory raises some serious problems. He does not explain how theoretical explanations even in the personal idiom can develop at all in a closed society. One would have thought that in such a society it would have been enough to live with the received tradition. Put more simply: How can one correlate the concept of a body of theory with an attitude of the unawareness of alternatives? Does not the very concept of "theory" (at least in the sense of the postulation of unobservables) entail, analytically, the concept of "alternative theories?" After all, if I am trying to explain the world, in my idiom, by the development of a theory, I must already be aware that I am developing a conjecture and that such a conjecture could be right or wrong and that other conjectures are possible.

There is another problem, an empirical one, namely, ethnography is replete with evidence that alternative theories do exist in so-called closed societies. Horton's own work shows this. In fact, Horton's concept of "secondary elaboration" was invented by him to explain precisely such evidence. But is not this concept itself an example of such a technique by an anthropologist in order to maintain a distinction between closed and open societies?

Further, to believe that the world stands in need of explanation already contains the possibility that the explanations are as likely to be false as they are to be true. To think at all means to think reflectively. But Horton wants to say both that traditional worldviews are logically elaborated, eminently rational, and, yet, that they contain no reflection about the general rules of thought. What Horton does not seem to realize is that even if one were to grant that such "second-order" conceptual activities were not institutionalized in traditional societies, this would not entail that such activity did not at least implicitly occur and that, therefore, the concept of alternatives would not be present. Just as one does not need the second-order knowledge of grammatical rules in order to speak grammatically, so one does not need the second-order knowledge of logical rules to be logical in one's thought. Unless Horton can demonstrate that "being logical" does not include the notion of awareness of alternatives, his case cannot stand.

Now, if in fact, despite the aforementioned objections, Horton has identified a system of thought which is explicitly not falsifiable in intent or content, perhaps the formal continuity is not a formal continuity at all but a different kind of cognitive venture than explanation. (We shall discuss this alternative in the second section of this chapter.) But this would involve the development of a theory of the nature of mythic thought, which permits the identification of different cognitive structures. There is, after all, no compelling reason why we should make thought and explanation equivalent concepts and then have to appeal to attitudes to account for any idiomatic differences. What Horton has done is to make the line of demarcation between scientific thought and religious thought dependent upon the criterion of falsifiability as suggested by Karl Popper (1963). Very few contemporary philosophers of science would acknowledge such a line of demarcation.

While we can be grateful to Horton for attacking what he calls the well-worn dichotomies such as intellectual versus emotional, rational versus mystical, reality oriented versus fantasy oriented, causally oriented versus supernaturally oriented, empirical versus nonempirical, and abstract versus concrete, and while we are happy that he has granted to religious thought in general, and mythic thought in particular, conceptual status, we cannot ignore his failure to account for the obvious differences between these kinds of thought. We think that Horton's mistake was settling for the concept of myth as explanation to begin with.

The Theory of Conceptual Relativism

Another form of this new explanatory theory of myth is that whether one is talking about myth or ritual, magical or religious belief, or any other form of human thought and activity, one cannot identify such conceptual systems as irrational, prelogical, mere expressions of emotion, or even false, because *all* thought, *all* logic, and *all* truth claims are culturally specific and contextually determined. Unlike Horton, who emphasizes idiomatic differences accompanied by different attitudes, this position focuses upon what it means for something to be identified as a conceptual system. Often accompanying this approach is the view that a radical distinction must be made between the natural and the social sciences, or, more generally, between the study of the world, and the study of human life and thought. In this approach, whereas all-natural science is the investigation of regularities understood as laws, the study of human life and thought requires a special method of inquiry, which pays attention to conceptually acquired rules distinguishable from natural laws. Human behavior is rule governed and, therefore, requires rule analysis rather than causal analysis. In this approach, the influence of the tradition of deflection in general, and the work of Weber in particular, is present.

One of the most articulate representatives of this general position, especially as it applies to the understanding of religion (and its mythic and ritualistic components), is the philosopher Peter Winch. Both in *The Idea of a Social Science and Its Relation to Philosophy* and in "Understanding a Primitive Society," Winch has eloquently argued for a new way of understanding religious thought and a new method for accomplishing that objective.

His argument is as follows: a philosophical (i.e., conceptual) analysis of social science will demonstrate that social relations between people include concepts. In fact, one can go so far as to say that human relations *are* conceptual relations. Social relations exist only in and through the ideas of people. This means that an analysis of social relations would not be a causal one. More importantly, this fact precludes the scientist from making cross-cultural and cross-linguistic generalizations about either the form or the content of the various kinds of human conceptual activity. It also prevents him from making judgments about the rationality of such conceptual activity.

"What is real and what is unreal shows itself in the sense that language has. Further, both the distinction between the real and the unreal, and the concept of agreement with reality themselves, belong to our language." Ontological, epistemological, methodological, theoretical, and even logical distinctions belong to our language. Contradictions can occur *within* any particular linguistic or cultural framework but not *between* or *among* such frameworks. No universal statements are possible. Therefore, the task in understanding societies in which myths or rituals occur is little more than tracing connections to be found within the specific conceptual schemes in which they occur. Each society, like each game, and each language, is complete within itself. So, the Azande in his myth and magic is making sense out of life; he is attempting to explain it in his own terms. "He and I are both thinking in patterns of thought provided for us by the societies in which we live" (1964: 80). There is no way of adjudicating between different conceptions of reality. It is within the use of language that religious conceptions have their place. The same applies to scientific concepts.

Although Winch has denied that such an approach is relativistic, it is difficult to make sense of his assertions in any other way for he has clearly relativized all concepts to the scheme in which they occur and made it impossible for any kind of translation from one scheme to another, or for any kind of cross-schematic generalizations.

The outcome of the theory of conceptual relativism is that mythical thought is granted conceptual status and is clearly distinguished from emotion, irrationality, or the esoteric, but, against Horton, it cannot be compared with or related to scientific thought. Such comparison would be possible only within the system of meanings characteristic of scientific thought. "Concepts used by primitive people [and concepts used by scientific people] can only be interpreted in the context of the way of life of these people" (Winch 1964: 95).

The position of conceptual relativism fails to be convincing for a number of reasons. Gellner has characterized it as the position of "conceptual charity." If in fact myths are explanations of the world and we are interested in explaining the world, then I see no reason why we cannot judge their truth and adequacy. The alternative is to suggest that "anything goes" as, in fact, Paul Feyerabend has recommended.

Furthermore, Winch's position is not an explanation of myths and rituals, including the problem of their rationality (Wilson 1970), but rather a recommendation as to how different systems of concepts should be treated and respected because we are all bound by our sociocultural matrix. Such a position leads to the death of scientific inquiry.

Third, the conceptual relativist also faces the problem of the status of his own claims. Either he is appealing to a metalinguistic or metacultural theory in terms of which he makes the judgments about the self-containment of

EXPLANATION OF MYTH, MYTH AS EXPLANATION

conceptual systems or he is not. If he is, then he has contradicted himself; the claims are, after all, universal, not bound by culture and language. If he is not, then he has solipsistically sealed himself into the kind of cave that permits neither entry nor exit of meaningful and true claims. How does Winch know that we cannot say what is in accord with reality? Where did such a criterion to make *that* judgment come from? How are we to evaluate Winch's claims? Or even understand them? Are there any bridges to his statements? If there are, how do we account for these movements from our conceptual schemes to his?

One of the most penetrating criticisms of conceptual relativism has recently been written by Roger Trigg (1973). Trigg starts by showing that a fundamental distinction must be drawn between the way the world is and what we say about it, even if we all happen to agree, *because we could all be wrong*. Agreement guarantees nothing. The logic of assertion includes the distinction between the world and claims about the world. This means that truth, as a regulative ideal, is built into the very structure of assertorical speech. To say "It is raining outside" commits one to having a notion of an outside and whether or not your claim can be applied. Even a conclusive verification of the claim that it is raining makes no difference, for the claim entails the distinction between the way the world is and what we say about the world. The conceptual relativist does not allow for the possibility that beliefs can be judged by measuring them against anything external to the beliefs. But then the relativist cannot make claims at all. And he could never make either true or false statements (whether he could *know* that the statements are true or false is a different issue). "We could all be wrong" entails that there is a regulative ideal in terms of which error can be judged—even if, in fact, we can never apply this criterion. If we say that every conceptual system is relative to the society in which it occurs, we face the problem of identifying a conceptual system in a society other than our own. How would we know how to apply the concept of "conceptual system?" If we claim that we *can* identify conceptual systems in other societies (and Winch speaks quite freely about Azande concepts), by what means do we do this? Trigg makes clear that the concept of commitment or arbitrary decision is of no help at all, for all commitments involve beliefs which are potentially true or false. Even if we grant that some beliefs are true only within the particular society, the question can still be asked about commitments to a system of beliefs. To appeal to the beliefs within the system to support a commitment to the system is circular. And to admit to beliefs external to the system in terms of which such commitments can be made is to move beyond relativism.

Winch has paid too high a price in order to grant to other systems of thought the dignity which they obviously deserve. His arguments clearly demonstrate why a scientific theory of myths similar in form to a scientific theory of anything in the world is both desirable and necessary. They also demonstrate why such a bitter battle exists within the social sciences between those who believe that scientific explanations of human life and thought are both possible and desirable and those who believe that they are impossible and unnecessary.

The Theory of Rational Dualism

The unpalatable consequences of conceptual relativism have been responsible for a closer examination on the part of both philosophers and social scientists of the question of whether alternative standards of rationality do exist. Winch's work was so powerfully argued that it gave rise to what has now become known as "the great rationality debate."

Steven Lukes (1967) is a philosopher-social scientist who has entered the fray. He attempts to give Lucifer his due. While his subject matter, like Horton's and Winch's, includes more than myths (in fact religion simply provides the occasion for discussing fundamental methodological questions about the nature and scope of scientific inquiry), it obviously has implications for more specific theories about the characterization of mythic systems and their explanation. He suggests that a number of alternative ways of characterizing mythic beliefs are possible and, in fact, have been adopted by scholars. Mythic beliefs may be thought of as symbolic, incomprehensible, explanatory, mystical, and contextually rational. In Lukes's view before we can discuss the problem of whether or not myths are explanations, we must first discuss whether or not they are rational, for the position of conceptual relativism is that if we conceive myths to be rational, and if we admit that logic and rationality are contingent, then we must admit that myths are correct rational explanations because there are no necessary or universal criteria in terms of which to judge them wrong. Lukes then proceeds to argue that some criteria of rationality are universal, that is, relevantly applicable to all beliefs in any context, while other criteria are particular, context dependent, and only relevantly applicable to beliefs in that context. The question then becomes how beliefs, such as mythic ones, are to be judged. What is involved here is the argument that we cannot understand the language of another culture, including its myths, unless we admit to a common reality for them and for us. Here Lukes is in agreement with Trigg. Further, we must admit that another culture's concepts of truth and falsity intersect with ours in at least some significant respects or else we could neither understand nor reject their claims. The language in the other culture would have to have operable logical rules such as the concepts of negation, identity, inference, and noncontradiction. Otherwise, we could never understand anything they say.

EXPLANATION OF MYTH, MYTH AS EXPLANATION

Lukes then admits that some utterances are obviously context dependent in the sense that they get meaning from their context. "There are obviously context-dependent criteria of meaning. Again, there are contextually provided criteria which make particular beliefs appropriate in particular circumstances. There are also contextually provided criteria which specify the best way to arrive at and hold beliefs. In general, there are contextually provided criteria for deciding what counts as a 'good reason' for holding a belief" (211). Particular myths, for example, would make sense because there are contextually provided criteria for evaluating such beliefs *within their context.*

A problem arises, however, when we ask questions not merely about beliefs in their context and according to their internal relations (and no one in this debate wishes to deny the obvious point that beliefs are internally related to other beliefs) but about the truth conditions for such beliefs. Lukes has already argued that there must be some universal elements involved. If myths are to be understood as making explanatory claims about the world, then they must conform to the universal canons of making truth claims. Contingent logic is subject to universal logic, for the latter specifies the ultimate constraints to which thought is subject. Lukes then proceeds to argue that all the versions he has suggested for characterizing mythic beliefs possess some validity. To identify mythic language as symbolic is partially right because some allowance must be made for contextual interpretation, and one way of distinguishing symbolic thought from literal thought is that symbolic thought is contextual thought, whereas literal thought is that kind of thought which is subject to the universal canons of logic. And to identify myths as incomprehensible is partly correct insofar as one judges them according to such universal canons. And to identify myths as explanations is partially right insofar as one recognizes that myths do make universal claims. This gives us the opportunity to assert their falsity.

The upshot of all of this is that in the evaluation and analysis of mythic thought we are left with two sets of analysis. The first method enables us to say that they are rational and either true or false explanations of the world. The second method enables us to say that within their context and according to their own mode they make sense. Lukes has made room for both Horton and Winch. But two wrongs don't make a right.

In following the intricacies of the foregoing argument, the reader might have forgotten that we have not been treated to an explanation of myth as explanation but only to the proposition that if myths are explanations, then there are two sets of criteria in terms of which they can be judged and evaluated. But we do not have to treat the assumption that myths are explanations of the world as a scientific, testable, hypothesis. We might very well simply treat it as data to be explained in some more powerful theory, which subsumes their explanatory form under more inclusive sets of ideas about the formal properties of mythic systems.

The Theory of Situational Logic

I. C. Jarvie (1969) is refreshingly explicit about myths. They are

> theories, hypotheses, conjectures, guesses—I use these words interchangeably. All theories are the result of trying to solve a problem. For example, Cargo cult doctrines are hypotheses to explain the problem, "what is white society and how does it get the wonderful material things it has?" The theories explain where these came from and how. The theories lead to viewing certain actions as being appropriate to call forth the required goods for black society as well. These actions, when performed, or rather these consequences, constitute tests of the theories on the basis of which they are performed. (123)

He also says: "Religion, it seems to me, is a set of theories or myths. *The function of all theories is to explain something.* In the case of religion, the problem to be solved is big: the world. Most religions claim to explain the origins, ground plan, building materials, and working of the world; often they also prescribe conduct" (66). Jarvie clearly conceives of myths as explanations; he assumes them to be such and then proceeds to say that the people who believe in them and use them in their reasoning are justified in doing so on the basis of the state of their knowledge.

Jarvie believes that the logic of myth and scientific theory are identical. This approach permits him to reject any view which characterizes myth as irrational. But it is also clear that this approach, assuming as it does the explanatory interpretation of myth, places religion in its "mythic" expression in direct conflict with science and its "theoretical" expression.

Now Jarvie is committed to situational logic as the basis from which the scholar is to understand and explain myth. Situational logic proposes that the reasons why people think what they think and do what they do can be rationally reconstructed. Upon such a reconstruction it will become apparent that odd modes of thought and odd styles of behavior are only *apparently* odd. They cease to be odd when the reasons for such thought and behavior are disclosed. Situational logic is an answer to the question: Why are these people acting and thinking in this way? People's theories and beliefs influence their actions, hence an analysis of the actions of people without reference to their beliefs will fail to explain the actions. He illustrates this approach in the following manner: The answer to "Why do some Englishmen worship God is 'because they believe there is a supreme and all-powerful being called "God" who demands to be worshiped.'" "It is no answer to that question to talk about the social structure of England. Of course, some people go to church for social rather than religious reasons. But this only illustrates the futility of studying the ritual and not the belief. The belief of a man is part of his situation" (219).

All of this becomes even clearer when one realizes that Jarvie is a methodological individualist rather than a methodological holist. As Alan Ryan (1973) points out, individualists explain human action on the basis of the individual beliefs of people. Social structures are derivable from individual structures; that is, social institutions consist of nothing more than the aggregation of individual beliefs and acts. Holists argue that what individuals do is the consequence of their place in social wholes (10). Individualists, therefore, tend to interpret social structures in psychological terms and holists tend to interpret psychological facts in social terms. Both approaches are reductionistic, but the reductions are in opposite directions. It is not surprising therefore that Jarvie views myths as explanations, because if a myth is a theory of the world, then obviously when one asks why a particular individual has the beliefs he has, and acts as he does, one will not look for causes beyond the individual (say in the sociocultural situation) but to his *reasons,* thus interpreting myth as rational explanatory activity.

Jarvis's (1969) position is very similar to Horton's and this is not particularly surprising because both derive a great deal of inspiration from the social philosophy of Karl Popper. They do differ in emphasis, however, for whereas Horton emphasizes the type of society in which different attitudes determine the idiom in which theories are developed, Jarvie emphasizes the role that reasons play in action.

Jarvis's position of situational logic is a coherent one and provides the basis for a falsifiable theory of myth but is not particularly interesting. We already know, before we read Jarvie, that people at least sometimes have reasons for what they think and do. But what Jarvie fails to explain is why people have *mythic* reasons. By identifying myth and explanatory theories to begin with, he can hardly end anywhere else. But what scientific theory has made such an identity plausible?

If we have learned anything from the painstaking work of ethnographers, it is that all human beings have an interest in explanations. Why not label the institutionalization of such explanatory interests science? (This is what anthropologists as diverse in their methods and theories as Malinowski and Levi-Strauss do.) What then needs to be explained is why mythic systems develop contrapuntally with explanatory systems and how such mythic systems can be characterized.

Structuralism

There is one scholar, Claude Levi-Strauss, working within the boundaries of the intellectualist tradition, who has not identified myths as a kind of explanation. "In order to understand what a myth really is, must we," he asks rhetorically, "choose between platitude and sophism? Some claim that human societies merely express, through their mythology, fundamental feelings common to the whole of mankind, such as love, hate, or revenge." This expressivist approach Levi-Strauss dismisses out of hand. "[Some claim] that they try to provide some kind of explanations for phenomena which they cannot otherwise understand" (1976: 203). Levi-Strauss refuses to accept this explanatory alternative because ethnographic studies have shown that all human societies are acquainted with empirical explanations. He finds it difficult to understand why such societies would attempt to explain the world in such elaborate and devious ways when they already have empirical explanations at hand. Something else besides explanations appears to be going on in myth even when some aspects of myths have an explanatory form.

Levi-Strauss, then, proposes a theory of myth, which subsumes their occasional explanatory content under broader and more inclusive theoretical concepts. In the process, he makes a theoretical advance, which contributes to a greater understanding of the nature of myth. How does he accomplish this?

Levi-Strauss defines his project as a theoretical description of the formal properties of mythic systems. He is able to accomplish this task by utilizing the kinds of models that had already been developed by Ferdinand de Saussure Sauand R. Jakobson. From Saussure he takes the distinction between structure (or system) and the exemplification of the system in particular concrete instances. (Saussure 1966) developed this distinction in order to differentiate between language [as a system of possible relationships] and speech [as the actualization of such relationships in real human social situations].) From Jakobson he takes the theory of how phonological rules operate in the formation of meaningful units (words or morphemes). He develops the hypothesis that underlying particular myths there lies a system of relationships very similar to the kind of structure underlying acts of human speech. Thus, we can develop a theory of the structure of myth along lines similar to a theory of the structure of language. Levi-Strauss is so taken with this idea that he even identifies myths as a kind of language (1963: 206). Just as particular words are composed of units which, in isolation, mean nothing (they are nothing more than sounds), so particular myths are composed of constituents which are meaningless in isolation. Only when the relationships between the units are specified does the meaning become apparent (1963: 207).

This approach has relevance for the problem of explanation, for if an explanatory episode occurs in a myth this is meaningless because it must be related to the system of which it is merely a constituent.

There is more at stake, however. Levi-Strauss wishes to "enlarge the framework of our logic to include processes which, whatever their

EXPLANATION OF MYTH, MYTH AS EXPLANATION

apparent differences, belong to the same kind of intellectual operation [as other intellectual operations]." He wishes to place myth squarely within the framework of the intellect, thus agreeing with the rationalists about the general cognitive character of myth, but unlike Horton, for example, who sees only a difference of idiom between mythic thought and scientific thought, Levi-Strauss sees a rigorous logic at work, but a logic applied to different objects and for different purposes.

What kind of a system is it, then, that characterizes myth? *Myth is a system of homologies.* Myths exist because human beings have discovered the conceptual and practical importance of developing elaborate taxonomies. Such taxonomies have the canonical form A:B::C:D (there are, however, variations of this form) and they proceed from the classification of the most specific and concrete details of everyday life to the most abstract concepts. Using another device derived from linguistic theory, Levi-Strauss distinguishes between the surface and the deep structure of myth. Discovering the underlying taxonomy at work involves considerable and painstaking analysis of particular myths and their many variants. Such depth analysis, then, will disclose the invariant features of myth. The surface features encode information which needs to be decoded by the proper structuralist techniques.

Levi-Strauss is quite clear that structuralism will not provide a causal explanation of myth. He says:

> Several among us hold more modest views on the future of social anthropology than those fostered by Radcliffe-Brown's great ambitions. They do not picture social anthropology modeled after the inductive sciences as they were conceived in the nineteenth century but rather see it as a taxonomy whose purpose is to identify and classify types, to analyze their constituent parts, and to establish correlations between them. (1976: 12)

And this is what Levi-Strauss proceeds to do with his mythic subject matter (thereby, with considerable irony, making social anthropology a form of mythology). Having established that myths are systems of homologies, he then proceeds to show that particular mythic systems have transformational relationships to each other.

What Levi-Strauss has not realized (at least in his published works) is that if he has indeed been successful in providing a theoretical description of the formal properties of mythic systems, then a major breakthrough has occurred in the scientific investigation of myths which can lead to genuine empirical cognitive work. This is a matter which I develop in my planned book *On the Acquisition, Structure and Function of Symbolic Systems* so I shall not discuss it at any length here except to say that such a theoretical advance occurred in the field of linguistics when, after Noam Chomsky (1957) had successfully described the formal properties of language systems in *Syntactic Structures* and *Aspects of a Theory of Syntax, (1964)* psycholinguists and sociolinguists were able to make significant empirical progress in the areas of language acquisition and language functions. There is no reason why such progress cannot now be made in empirical studies in the field of religion in general and myth and ritual in particular. We may be on the verge of finally developing causal explanations of religious behavior of a genuinely theoretical kind without having to settle for outmoded models including models which accept myths at their face value (Horton 1970: 152).

Levi-Strauss has been interested in developing not only a theory of the *structure* of myth but also a theory of the *meaning* of myth. The influence of Saussure on this aspect of his work is very powerful. Saussure had conceived of the science of semiology, that is, a general science of signs and symbols and Levi-Strauss conceives of the task of social anthropology as being directly concerned with some of these systems of signs, for example, oral and ritual gestures, marriage rules, kinship systems, and so on (1976: 9). Using the linguistic model (or at least the phonological component of the linguistic model), Levi-Strauss attempts to show that just as meaningless sounds are combined to form meaningful words, so meaningless mythic and ritual constituents are combined to form meaningful homologies. Myths then are viewed as a system of meanings, a semantic system. Unfortunately, as Sperber (1964) has shown, this is the weakest aspect of Levi-Strauss's theoretical model, for any natural language consists of three components, the phonological, the syntactic, and the semantic. There is no way in which one can derive a semantic theory, even by analogy, from a phonological theory. What Levi-Strauss has shown is that myths are *structured.* His assertion that the meaning of myth is the structure of myth does not make sense for it is like saying that the meaning of language is the phonological structure of language. However, this aspect of Levi-Strauss's theory is not irreparable. Sperber has shown how the identification of myth as a system of homologies is significant in that it shows that myth is more like a system of knowledge than it is like a system of language. So even though using the linguistic model has been useful in making the discovery of mythic structure possible (by identifying the rule-governed nature of myth), Levi-Strauss has in fact discovered a genuinely cognitive structure, distinct from linguistic structures. Rather than identifying myth as a species of language (Lawson 1976) having the special properties of a semantic system, we now have the means for identifying myth as a species of knowledge, that is, having the special properties of a cognitive system. Therein lies its power.

If Levi-Strauss is right, that is, if his theory has application to problems such as the acquisition and function of symbolic systems, then we may be able to

EXPLANATION OF MYTH, MYTH AS EXPLANATION

explain the persistence of myth even in the context of the development and institutionalization of science. Encoded in myth is a kind of implicit knowledge (not a kind of language), which is so important to human beings that to attempt to eradicate it would involve a change in what it means to be human. For what we are now dealing with is a special kind of human capacity, which is a part of our very makeup.

One thing is certain. The answer to the question "What are myths, what do they mean (if they mean anything), what do they tell us about human capacities?" will not wait for a collection and collation of all the myths in the world. Just as linguistic theory did not wait for a collection of all the sentences that had ever been spoken in every language before the theoretical advances made in transformational-generative grammar, so mythic theory (and the much larger theory of religion) does not have to wait until all the data has been gathered. In fact, as the intellectualist tradition has realized, the problem is not of the inductive sort (hence the lively interdisciplinary debate between philosophers and social scientists described earlier). It is a time for bold theories about the formal properties of religious systems and the ingenuity to devise ways to find application for them to the welter of data which religionists have already gathered. But the data do not suggest the theories. Carl Hempel has said: "Scientific hypotheses and theories are not derived from observed facts, but invented in order to account for them. They constitute guesses at the connection that might obtain between phenomena under study, and the uniformities and patterns that might underlie the occurrences" (1966: 15). If any scholar in recent years has made this bold move it has been Levi-Strauss. Scholars in religion would do well to apply his theories to their subject matter and emulate his boldness.

References

Abel, Theodore F. (1948). "The Operation Called *Verstehen*," *American Journal of Sociology* 54: 211–18.
Bidney, David (1965). "Myth, Symbolism and Truth." (Cf. Sebeok: 3–23).
Brodbeck, M. (1968). *Readings in the Philosophy of Social Science*, New York: McMillan Co.
Chomsky, Noam (1957). *Syntactic Structures*, The Hague: Mouton and Co.
Chomsky, Noam (1964). *Aspects of the Theory of Syntax*, Cambridge, MA: The MIT Press.
Fontenrose, J. (1971). *The Ritual Theory of Myth*, Berkeley: University of California Press.
Gunner, Rolf (1967). "Understanding in the Social Sciences and History," *Inquiry* 10: 156–8.

Hempel, Carl G. (1966). *The Philosophy of Natural Science*, Englewood Cliffs: Prentice Hall.

Hempel, Carl G. (1968). "The Logic of Functional Analysis." (Cf. Brodbeck: 179–210).

Horton, Robin (1970). "African Traditional Thought and Western Science." (Cf. Wilson 131–71).

Jarvie, I. C. (1969). *The Revolution in Anthropology*, Chicago: Henry Regnery Company.

Lawson, E Thomas (1976). "Ritual as Language Religion," *A Journal of Religion and Religions* 6: 123–39.

Levi-Strauss, Claude (1963). *Structural Anthropology*, Garden City: Doubleday and Company.

Levi-Strauss, Claude (1976). *Structural Anthropology*, vol. II, New York: Basic Books.

Lukes, Steven (1967). "Some Problems About Rationality." (Cf Wilson: 194–213).

Malinowski, B. (1948). *Magic, Science and Religion*, Garden City: Doubleday and Company, Inc.

Penner, Hans H. (1971). "The Poverty of Functionalism," *History of Religions* 23 (4): 372–81.

Popper, Karl (1963). *Conjectures and Refutations*, New York Harper and Row.

Rudner, Richard (1966). *The Philosophy of Social Science*, Englewood Cliffs: Prentice Hall.

Ryan, Allan (1973). *The Philosophy of Social Science*, Englewood Cliffs: Prentice Hall.

de Saussure, Ferdinand (1966). *A Course m General Linguistics*, New York: McGraw Hill.

Skorupski, John (1976). *Symbol and Theory: A Philosophical Study of Theories of Religion in Social Anthropology*, Cambridge: Cambridge University Press.

Sperber, Dan (1964). *Rethinking Symbolism*, Cambridge: Cambridge University Press.

Trigg, Roger (1973). *Reason and Commitment*, Cambridge: Cambridge University Press.

Wilson, Bryan (1970). *Rationality*, New York: Harper and Row.

Winch, Peter (1958). *The Idea of a Social Science and Its Relation to Philosophy*, London: Routledge and Kegan Paul.

Winch, Peter (1964). "Understanding a Primitive Society" (Cf. Wilson: 78–111).

INTRODUCTION TO CHAPTER 8

The process of natural selection shapes organic design. Any organism that is capable of distinguishing agents from everything else has an evolutionary advantage. An agent is an organism that is capable of intentional action. All kinds of things follow from this fact and explain the remarkable success of Homo sapiens sapiens *and perhaps its final conflagration in some future cataclysm of global warming and nuclear destruction.*

8

Psychological Perspectives on Agency

In previous work (Lawson and McCauley 1990), we showed that our theory of religious ritual competence makes substantive predictions about an array of features concerning religious rituals. We also argued that the representation of religious *ritual* action depends upon general cognitive mechanisms for the representation of action. We maintained that the representation of action requires the notion of agency, that the notion of agency involves the notion of agents in action, that such actions either may or may not involve patients, that our technical notion of religious ritual action requires the notion of patients, and, finally, that what distinguishes religious ritual actions from actions of all other kinds is that agents who appear in the structural descriptions of religious rituals possess special qualities. Aside from this notion of special qualities, the structural descriptions of religious ritual action typically possess the same features as do representations of ordinary actions.

Focusing upon the representation of action highlights both the continuities and differences between ritual action and actions of other kinds. The representation of an ordinary action, for example, a man washing a baby with water, would include information such as the facts that the man functions as the agent, washing is the action the agent performs, the baby occupies the role of the patient of the action, and water is the instrument. How does this representation differ from that of a religious ritual in which a priest baptizes a baby with water? On nearly all fronts, not very much. This religious ritual employs the same basic representational structure: A does B to C by means of D. What makes this example of a religious ritual action noteworthy is that its structural description involves an agent (in this case a priest) who possesses a special quality (being ordained) in order to be able to perform the ritual action (baptism) upon a patient (the baby) by means of water (which possesses a special quality by virtue of having been consecrated previously). The parenthetical information will vary from tradition to tradition, but the structure remains the same—someone does something to somebody (or something), often by means of something. The differences turn exclusively on the peculiarities of religious conceptual schemes.

Here, I argue that religious representations, while obviously cultural in content, rest on noncultural foundations of the sort outlined by our theory. The first half of this chapter shows that theoretical and experimental work in cognitive, developmental, and evolutionary psychology supports our theory's prediction that: (1) humans have special resources for representing agents and their actions and (2) the acquisition of many key features of symbolic-cultural systems, like religious ritual systems, requires neither detailed instruction nor even extensive learning about elaborate cultural models. The second half of this chapter argues that additional empirical findings from recent experimental studies in cognitive psychology corroborate our theory's claim that subjects (1) will have converging intuitions about the well-formedness of religious rituals; (2) will appreciate the central importance of superhuman agency in the representation of religious rituals; and (3) will judge the specialness of culturally postulated superhuman agents (henceforth CPS agents) as the most important factor in a religious ritual's success or failure, their lack of familiarity with most of the relevant religious system's details notwithstanding.

Resources for Representing Agents and Their Actions

Not only is the theory McCauley and I advanced in *Rethinking Religion* (1990) supported by recent theories of cognitive structure and development, but in turn, it also supports such theorizing. Our theory, for example, describes a specialized action-representation system (henceforth ARS) that humans possess for representing subsets of entities (i.e., agents) and events (i.e., actions) in the world. It also makes predictions about how such a system is exploited for religious purposes. Our theory, however, says nothing about the age at which such a system is operative. If we were to discover that even very young children have command of these distinctions about agents and their actions, then it would seem uncontroversial that adults also have access to such resources. (Meltzoff and Moore 1994) Additionally, if it turned out that young children did have command of such distinctions, then this fact would also permit us to deal with issues concerning the extent to which the noncultural foundations of some forms of knowledge need to be taken into account when dealing with issues concerning the role of instruction in the transmission of knowledge.

In *Rethinking Religion,* we already had argued that, by virtue of such cognitive underpinnings, the acquisition of symbolic-cultural systems such as religious systems does not depend upon extensive instruction concerning the details of elaborate cultural models. The knowledge in question is mostly tacit. We illustrated this, in fact, by showing how, in an informal experiment, subjects were able to specify properties of nonexistent religious rituals, for example, a ritual of divorce. The fact that they were able to do so implied that they had command of a tacit system of knowledge that enabled them to make judgments about the kinds of agents required in such a ritual, the qualities of the agents involved, the number of agents required, and the types of acts that would be necessary for a ritual of divorce to be successful. We thought that such tacit systems of knowledge were underdetermined by cultural input and by instruction in particular, but we did not, in our earlier work, make an explicit appeal to empirical studies in psychology and anthropology. I intend to do so now.

If the developmental evidence shows, as I think that it does, that an ARS is present at an early age, then this would explain why symbolic-cultural systems pivotally do not depend upon instruction for their persistence. In fact, the ARS seems to play a fundamental role in the acquisition of specific cultural contents such as religious concepts (see Figure 8 in chapter 5 of *Rethinking Religion* for the relationship between conceptual schemes and the ARS). While we did not develop an explicit theory of cultural transmission in *Rethinking Religion,* I do think that the theory we advanced there is readily subject to fruitful elaboration by psychologists and anthropologists of religion. Certainly, more and more theoretical and empirical work in this area is currently underway.

Cultural transmission is of considerable theoretical interest because it involves questions about why some representations are successfully transmitted while others seem to disappear. I think that the cognitive variables highlighted by our theory impinge in important ways upon the processes that account for the transmission of culture. This is illustrated by the pivotal, systematic connections between issues of memory and the variables our theory isolates concerning the character and location of CPS agents in the representations of religious rituals (see chapter 5 of *Rethinking Religion*). I am concerned with how our theory connects with issues of transmission in terms of the types of cognitive and developmental considerations I explore in the first half of this chapter. This is not a simple story; I shall consider some selectionist ideas discussed by Pascal Boyer (1994, 1998), place these in a general evolutionary framework, and examine evidence from cognitive, developmental, and social psychology.

In elaborating and defending a theory concerning the transmission of religious systems, Pascal Boyer (1994, 1998) has, in effect, confirmed most of the central commitments of the theory we developed in *Rethinking Religion*. This does not mean to imply that Boyer's theory goes no further than ours does. To the contrary, he has developed an account of religious transmission that explores a wide range of issues our theory does not address. Nevertheless, Boyer emphasizes the prominence of selectionist considerations in explaining the cognitive foundations of the transmission and persistence of symbolic-cultural systems such as religions. Some religious representations simply are more easily learned, more easily remembered, and more easily communicated than are others. However, the critical point is that, due to the character of our cognitive systems, some representations are better candidates for selection than others are. Boyer suggests that good candidates exemplify a cognitively optimal balance between intuitive properties that are easily remembered (in fact he argues that they should be regarded as default assumptions) and counterintuitive, attention-grabbing properties.

In discussing "a cognitive catalog of the supernatural," Boyer notes that the concept of an intentional agent is probably the most frequently manipulated category in religious ontologies. He also observes that this category is fundamental to the intuitive background assumptions that make so much about CPS agents so readily comprehensible, despite their counterintuitive qualities. Of course, it is just these features of agency and action that our theory's claims about the ARS capture.

In examining the noncultural foundations of religious ritual representations, especially since these involve the notion of agency, we need to examine the relationship between the representation of religious ritual actions and also the representation of actions generally. Human beings clearly seem to possess the cognitive resources needed to represent action. If it is true, as I have already claimed, that these resources include an ARS capable of being employed for religious ritual purposes, then the opportunity arises to examine the conditions of such a system's emergence, together with the ways in which it suits religious purposes. We need, in other words, to account for its presence and to describe its use. This is where the long-term view of evolutionary theory intersects with the short-term account of cognitive structure and development, that is, where theories of phylogeny intersect theories of ontogeny. The evolutionary story concerning how human brains developed the way they did inevitably will constrain the ontogenetic story of the development of human cognitive abilities.

Evolutionary theory shows how the process of natural selection shapes organic design. From an evolutionary perspective, it certainly seems as if creatures with the kind of mental equipment specified by an ARS capable of distinguishing between agents and everything else would possess an adaptive advantage. Possessing the cognitive wherewithal to distinguish between agents and everything else means possessing the representational resources to detect such agents and to attend to the actions they perform.

Survival in a complex world, both natural and social, clearly would be facilitated by the recognition of agents and their actions. For their own good, creatures with this ability must be able to tell the difference between mom and a breadbox. Both possess important resources, but only mom is able to deliver them on demand. Similarly, our prehistoric ancestors had to be able to distinguish leopards from logs rapidly, or they would have served as the leopard's lunch. Human commerce with the world requires complex representation of agents and their actions in order to facilitate negotiations with the many types of entities present in the environment, whether for the purposes of gaining resources or in order to avoid predators.

A number of psychologists and anthropologists have proposed evolutionary accounts for the organization and structure of the human mind. Some of these accounts have attempted to show how such theories of mind are applicable to religious ideas and practices (Pyysiainen). Barkow, Tooby, and Cosmides (1992), Sperber (1990), Boyer (1994), and Mithen (1996) have, for example, argued that the kinds of minds that we have today have resulted more from the process of natural selection than advocates of cultural learning typically have maintained. Because evolution takes a long time, there appears to be very little difference between the minds we have today and the minds our ancestors possessed a hundred thousand years ago. Essentially, our minds reflect our ancestors' adaptation to the Pleistocene period.

Although little about us seems to have changed, a paradox exists, since everywhere around us, we are confronted by an astonishing range of cultural variation and diversity. Cultural contents clearly differ across the globe. And as far as the historical record shows, such diversity has, if anything, accelerated through time. Such cultural variation requires explanation. If our minds have changed little since the Pleistocene period, why are their products so diverse?

This obvious diversity has led evolutionary thinkers interested in culture in general and religion in particular to argue about its depth. Is it variable all the way down, or will sophisticated analysis of sufficient complexity disclose a level of cognitive commonality beneath the surface? Religions are of particular interest here because historical and ethnographic studies present us with a bewildering variety of religious ideas and practices through time and across cultures. The diversity of religious representations provides us with a particularly fascinating case for investigation because it seems to present a major problem for those who wish to postulate the psychic unity of humankind. If we all have the same cognitive equipment, and we all must fulfill the same basic needs, why do we end up thinking so differently, especially in the realm of religious ideas?

The strategy cognitive scientists such as Boyer, Sperber (1975, 1996), and Mithen have employed in order to tease out the commonalities underlying such diversity in religious representations has been to attempt to specify the principles involved in cultural transmission. The dynamics of cultural transmission would appear to favor either replication or transformation. One way of dealing with such problems is by examining the cognitive dynamics of cultural transmission. And one of the things that we know about such dynamics is that some forms of knowledge are readily acquired, whereas other forms of knowledge come only with great difficulty (McCauley 1998, and this volume). For example, learning how to speak a language is easy for a young child, whereas learning how to employ calculus is hard work. What is there about the human mind that makes it predisposed to the rapid acquisition of some information and the slow and tedious acquisition of other forms of knowledge? For the purposes of this chapter, all we need to recognize is that human minds seem to be predisposed to acquire certain forms of knowledge with astonishing speed and to acquire other forms of knowledge with great difficulty. Of particular interest to us at this point is humans' predisposition to recognize and employ the notion of agency, a predisposition that opens the gates to conceptualizing agents with some extraordinary qualities.

Whether the predisposition to recognize agents early and easily is innate, requiring only certain triggers for its activation, or whether it is the consequence of a complex developmental process, is a fascinating question in its own right. Indeed, this question has generated considerable creative work in cognitive science, together with some rather acrimonious debates. Nevertheless, little that we wish to defend hangs upon the particular perspectives adopted by the contending parties (classical vs. connectionist) in this scholarly dispute. For example, Elman et al. (1996) represent one aspect of this dispute, in which Elman and his collaborators attempt to redefine classical approaches to issues about innateness, modularity, and domain specificity along connectionist lines. Jerry Fodor's *The Modularity of Mind* (1983) is an influential version of the classical account. In earlier work (1990), I and McCauley already have argued that the acquisition of symbolic-cultural systems such as religious systems, like natural languages, requires little if any explicit instruction and,

PSYCHOLOGICAL PERSPECTIVES ON AGENCY

therefore, rests considerably upon noncultural foundations. The transmission of these systems, especially throughout prehistory and in societies without the benefit of literacy, appears to turn largely on their natural cognitive appeal rather than on the mastery of elaborate cultural models that bear so much of the analytical burden in considerable work in cultural anthropology and the history of religions. Many cognitive features of religious materials, for example, their overwhelming reliance on narratives, render them the kind of cultural representations that human beings readily generate, learn, remember, and transmit. These materials' persistence suggests that the representational principles our theory isolates should prove cognitively salient; their ready and early acquisition suggests that those principles should arise early in cognitive development.

Generally, research on cognitive structure and development shows that human beings' perceptual systems seem especially attuned to detecting other human beings and distinguishing them from all other physical objects (Guthrie). People have a "theory" of the kinds of things that there are in the world and what to expect about such things. For example, infants who are four months old seem to have specific expectations about the cohesion and continuity of physical objects and the contact between them (Spelke 1991; Spelke, Phillips, and Woodward 1996 [1995]). Psychologists have designed experiments to gauge the reaction of infants to some rather strange phenomena such as one physical object passing through another. When one physical object apparently passes through another, infants exhibit a sense of surprise. Such an event contravenes infants' expectations about what physical objects can and cannot do because it provides evidence that is unexpected in infants' conception, or "theory," of the physical world. When the expectations generated by an infant's intuitive ontology are violated, the infant "can't believe its eyes!" and the length of its gaze indicates its reaction.

While infants do not expect physical objects to pass through one another and while they seem to express astonishment when they apparently do (by gazing at them for longer periods of time), they also expect physical objects to differ from each other in important respects. They seem to know that not all physical objects are alike, that is, that different objects possess different properties. For example, Premack (1990) argues that infants distinguish objects that move when acted upon from those that move on their own. In other words, infants seem to possess the notion of self-propelledness and to have command of its properties. When something moves that is not supposed to, it rivets their attention.

That infants have command of such concepts takes us near the threshold of the notion of agency, because we are dealing with a predisposition that permits infants to differentiate between motion as such and agent causation. Agents can cause themselves to move, and, by virtue of that capacity, they can cause other things to move as well. But while self-motion or self-propelledness is necessary for possessing a concept of agency, it is hardly sufficient and a number of cognitive scientists have proceeded to extend Premack's initial analysis. Alan Leslie (1996 [1995]) has developed Premack's notions and has attempted both to clear the conceptual landscape and to devise experiments to demonstrate the abilities of young children.

Clearing the Conceptual Landscape

Leslie (1996 [1995]) has made an important contribution to theoretical work about agency by approaching the problem in a particularly lucid and systematic way. He clears the ground by making the case for distinguishing the concept of agency from the concepts of causality and animacy notions that are often and easily conflated. For example, if we say that Tom broke the window by striking it with a hammer, we can mean that Tom is the cause of the window having been broken or that the hammer is the cause of the window having been broken or that Tom is the agent involved in the action of breaking the window. It may be tempting to conceive of either Tom or the hammer as an agent. But Leslie argues that, unless we are speaking or thinking metaphorically, we do not naturally come to think of hammers as agents. Humans are not naturally predisposed to think of hammers in terms of the notion of agency, even if hammers can be moved. So, Leslie argues, we need to be able to specify the difference between causality, animacy, and agency.

Why not argue that the notion of agency involves the notion of causation? By saying that Tom breaks the window, do we not identify Tom as at least one of the causes of the broken window? Leslie argues that there is more at stake in the notion of agency than the notion of causality. Causality typically involves such things as objects impinging on other objects, for example, people such as Tom and hammers breaking windows. Under such a description, both Tom and the hammer are physical and both are causes. But Leslie cautions us not to ignore the fact that there are important differences between hammers breaking windows and people breaking windows with hammers. In the case of the hammer breaking the window, all other factors being excluded, we are dealing with the notion of physical causality, which is a purely mechanistic notion. An earthquake can cause a hammer to bounce into the air, hit a window at the end of its trajectory, and, by such physical contact, break the glass in the window. Regarding the hammer as an agent is not necessary for comprehending this situation. All we need here is the notion of causality. What is interesting, of course, is that very young children seem to know the difference between people and other physical objects such as hammers. For them, there is more to Tom than physical causality. We could say that, because Tom is an agent, he requires a more complex representation than does a hammer.

Leslie also cautions theoreticians against confusing agency and animacy. Animacy typically involves conceiving of things as being capable of birth, growth, reproduction, and death. Possessing such a notion permits us to recognize the difference between kinds of physical objects, namely between those things that are alive and those that are not, such as people and hammers. Although many animate things are obviously capable of being characterized as agents and typically are, the fact that they are animate should not be confused with the fact that they are capable of being viewed as agents. Animacy is a necessary but not a sufficient condition for the notion of agency.

An Empirical Example

Before we summarize Leslie's constructive analysis of the distinguishing features of agency, we wish to show that his views are not simply the result of philosophical reflection but also are based upon experimental research. In a number of experiments (Leslie 1982, 1984, 1986, [1995]; Leslie and Keeble 1987), Leslie has shown that infants employ a complex concept of agency. For example, he argues (1996 [1995]) that six-month-old infants recognize the billiard ball "launching effect," which simply involves an event in which one billiard ball hits another billiard ball. Before we describe Leslie's experiment, we should know what his purpose was in performing it. Leslie designed the experiment to demonstrate that there is a level of representation basic to human intelligence that makes mechanical information explicit. If this claim is correct, according to Leslie, then Hume's attempt to eliminate mechanics from human understanding and replace it with the registration of spatiotemporal properties and the statistical association of spatiotemporal properties with one another is misleading. He agrees with Hume that humans see only spatiotemporal properties because vision involves explicit information about space and spatial arrangements over time. But Leslie thinks that Hume was wrong to argue that our idea of causation is based upon statistical association. "What makes launching seem 'perfect' to us as an instance of cause and effect is that it instantiates a mechanical interaction with a perfect transmission of 'FORGE'" (1996 [1995]: 124).

Leslie's experiment with the billiard ball launching effect proceeds as follows. The experimenters habituate a group of infants to a film of a direct launching event in which billiard ball number one rolls toward billiard number two and makes contact with it. Billiard ball number two moves upon contact. The experimenters habituate a second group of infants to a variation of the launching event by introducing a time delay of 0.5 seconds between the impact of number one on number two and the movement of number two. According to Leslie, Michotte (1963) already had demonstrated that when adults were presented with these two types of events, the interposition of the short delay destroyed the impression of causality in the first events. In the case of the infants, each group, after having been habituated to their respective events, was then shown the event to which they had become habituated in reverse, that is, by running the film backward. Running each film backward involves a change in both spatial direction and temporal order. In the film without the time delay, the pusher becomes the pushed (pushers are transmitters of FORGE and the pushed are its recipients). Reversing the film maintains this effect. However, there exists neither the pusher nor pushed when running the second film with the time delay backward. Reversing the film does not reverse the roles. Leslie concludes,

> If the infants construe these events from a mechanical point of view, then the direct launching event in reverse (film 1) will be more interesting than the non-causal delayed event in reverse. Therefore, even though the spatio-temporal changes and the contingency properties are equated in the test for the two groups, the causal group should recover attention more. This is exactly what we found. (1996 [1995]: 126)

What Leslie has shown is that, because of the role reversal, the subjects in the first experiment, after having been habituated to the billiard ball hitting another ball and causing it to move, will recover their attention when the film is reversed. The pushed becomes the pusher. In the second experiment, because of the time lag, there is no perception of causation. Thus, when the film is reversed, exactly the same thing happens as in the first film. Because there is no reversal of roles, there is nothing new to observe and no reason for the subject's interest to be revived.

Leslie's Constructive Views

If Leslie is right, then we have evidence that six-month-old infants already possess the concept of a physical object that possesses the property of transmittable FORGE from one physical object to another. This is one aspect of the *mechanical* element in the notion of agency. What we need, in addition, is the notion of an internal, renewable sense of FORGE. Leslie says:

> Because objects move as a result of force, and because Agents have an internal and renewable source of FORGE, Agents are free to move on their own—what Premack (1990) calls self-propelledness. Mere physical

> objects, however, lack an internal and renewable source of FORGE and therefore move only as a result of receiving FORGE externally from Agents or other objects that bear FORGE transiently. This simple FORGE dynamical assumption, relating patterns of motion to the force properties of the objects exhibiting the patterns, provides a powerful learning mechanism for the infants. (1996: 131)

In our cognitive repertoires, agents, though physical and therefore capable of acting as causes, and though animate, and therefore capable of actualizing all the properties of living things, are cognitively represented as a special type of physical object consisting of a number of unique properties. In Leslie's view, these are mechanical, actional (or teleological), and cognitive (or intentional).

As we have just seen in Leslie's experiment, agents contain mechanical properties by virtue of having an internal and renewable source of energy or "FORGE." In other words, what makes an agent different from a physical object such as a hammer is that agents are conceived of as possessing something "inside" that makes them capable of using the hammer. One way of describing this special property of an agent is to view the agent as having an "essence" that a hammer does not. Hammers do not have an internal renewable source of energy. If hammers move, they move only by virtue of something else moving them. Tom picks up the hammer. The hammer just lies there unless moved by something. Agents move because they have something inside them that causes them to be capable of moving. It is as if they have a special hidden engine. And this internal resource is regarded as an enduring rather than as a momentary property acquired by contact with something else.

Mechanical properties, however, are not sufficient to conceptualize the notion of agents. Agents also have actional (or teleological) properties. They simply do not move, nor do they move simply because they have an internal engine; rather, they act by pursuing goals. Agents act according to purposes. The lion feels hungry and wants some (gazelle) food. The lion's action of stalking the gazelle should be understood as purposeful action. And when we see the lion in action, we attribute to the lion this purpose. We know what the lion wants.

Finally, and most importantly, agents have cognitive (or intentional) properties, and their behavior is informed by such properties. To attribute intentionality to an agent is more than simply attributing purposes to the candidate for agency. Purposes are nonpropositional; they are not about anything. Intentions are propositional. So, if the lion were capable of representing "The gazelle is good food and knows that I regard him as a possible lunch" propositionally, we would say that the lion is capable of having purposes with propositional content and, in fact, is attributing intentionality to the gazelle. Of course, human beings do this every day, both to themselves

98   IMAGINING THE COGNITIVE SCIENCE OF RELIGION

and to other people. They even do it to animals. People adopt what Dennett (1987) has called the intentional stance, and they attribute both to themselves and to others a "Theory of Mind" (ToM) (see Carruthers and Smith 1996). As Baron-Cohen and Swettenham say:

> One of the most important achievements of modern developmental psychology has been to draw attention to the universal and astonishing capacity of young children to mind-read; it appears incontrovertible that by four years of age children interpret behavior in terms of agents' mental states . . . they mentalize: they convert the behavior they see others perform, or that they perform themselves, into actions driven by beliefs, desires, intentions, hopes, knowledge, imagination, pretense, deceit and so on. Behavior is instantly, even automatically, interpreted in terms of what the agent might be thinking, or planning, or wanting. (1996: 158)

So, what distinguishes the concept of agency from all of the other things in the world is that agents are physical, animate entities with renewable sources of energy, capable of acting according to purposes and with the capacity to attribute mental qualities to others.

Baron-Cohen (1995) has devised an even more sophisticated theory than Premack and Leslie by arguing that mind reading, which is fundamental to the attribution of agency, involves the interaction of four separate systems. Agreeing with Tooby and Cosmides (Barkow, Tooby, and Cosmides 1992) that natural selection has produced a mind-reading system, Baron-Cohen proposes a theory of four mechanisms that underlie the capacity of mind reading. These are an intentionality detector (henceforth ID), an eye-direction detector, a shared-attention mechanism, and a theory of mind mechanism. Working through vision, touch, and audition, the ID is a perceptual device that interprets motion stimuli in terms of the primitive, volitional, and mental states of goal and desire (Baron-Cohen 1995: 32). According to Baron-Cohen, to see anything animate moving, all that is required to interpret its movement is the attribution of goal and desire. X is moving because its goal is to go over there or because it wants something. Baron-Cohen argues that the ID is activated whenever there is any perceptual input that could identify something as an agent, or agent-like, for example, anything capable of self-propelled motion.

Baron-Cohen (1995: 35–8) cites four sources of evidence for the ID: (1) Reddy's (1991) experiments demonstrating that infants respond to the distinction between a give and a tease, thus showing that they are sensitive to changes in an adult's goal; (2) Heider and Simmel's (1944) discovery that subjects anthropomorphize geometrical objects that move around by describing them in terms of the actions of agents; (3) Perret and his colleagues' (Perret and Mistlin 1990; Hietanen and Perrett 1991) identification

PSYCHOLOGICAL PERSPECTIVES ON AGENCY

of cells in the temporal lobe of the monkey brain that respond selectively to the sight of another animal facing forward; and (4) Warrington and Shalice's (1984) discovery that some patients with focal brain damage lose the ability to employ the distinction between animate and inanimate objects.

The second mechanism that Baron-Cohen proposes is the eye-direction detector (henceforth EDD). Working only through vision, the EDD detects the presence and the direction of eyes or eye-like stimuli, and it infers that if another organism's eyes are directed at something, then that organism sees that thing. Baron-Cohen regards this function as particularly important because it permits the infant to attribute perceptual states to other organisms (1995: 38–9). The evidence for such a mechanism comes from the work of psychologists such as Daphne Maurer and her colleagues (Maurer and Barrera 1981: 39) who found that two-month-old infants looked almost as long at the eyes as at a whole face, but they looked far less at other parts of the face. In addition to detecting eyes, infants also are capable of detecting the direction of the eyes, that is, what the eyes are looking at. Six-month-olds look longer at someone looking at them than at someone looking away. The EDD also is capable of interpreting eyes looking at the subject as eyes "seeing" the subject, that is, whether the eyes are "looking at me" or "looking at not-me" (Maurer and Barrera 1981: 43).

These two mechanisms, the ID and the EDD, can construct dyadic representations such as agent wants X, agent has goal Y (in the case of ID); and agent sees X, and agent is looking at Y (in the case of EDD). From Baron-Cohen's point of view, they are not, however, sufficient to account for more complex representations such as agent A sees that agent B sees X. For such a representation Baron-Cohen argues that we need a shared-attention mechanism (henceforth SAM).

The SAM builds triadic representations that specify the relations among an agent, the self, and a (third) object, which can be another agent. Such triadic relations would have the form of "agent sees that I see X" or "you and I see that we are looking at the same object" (Baron-Cohen 1995: 45). Baron-Cohen adduces as evidence for the SAM, which is obviously dependent on the EDD, the gaze monitoring typical of nine-month-old infants (Scaife and Bruner 1975; Butterworth 1991). He claims that by fourteen months, children the world over engage in this activity. What happens is that the infant looks in the same direction as someone else looking at something and then it alters its gaze between the object being looked at and the person looking at the other object. Baron-Cohen also notes toddlers' finger-pointing behavior at this period of development. Evidently, the infant points with an outstretched finger at an object, then it alternates its gaze between the other person and the object at which the finger is pointed. Baron-Cohen argues that such behavior is effective in directing attention to a shared focal object (Baron-Cohen 1995:

48). The SAM, according to Baron-Cohen, also makes the ID's output available to the EDD. The importance of this is that it allows the EDD to interpret eye direction in terms of an agent's goal or desires.

Baron-Cohen postulates one additional mechanism, the theory of mind mechanism (henceforth ToM mechanism). Here, Baron-Cohen obviously is building upon the aforementioned work of Alan Leslie. Leslie's theory of agency distinguishes the mechanical, teleological, and intentional aspects of agency, but it does not contain the ID, EDD, or SAM mechanisms. Baron-Cohen believes that, while these additional mechanisms are necessary for developing an adequate account of the architecture of a theory of mind, they are not sufficient. A theory of mind also must involve the representation of epistemic mental states such as pretending, thinking, knowing, and believing, in which agents are represented as having attitudes toward propositions. It also must turn all of this mentalistic knowledge into a theory uniting mental states and actions.

As evidence for these two functions of the ToM mechanism, Baron-Cohen appeals to the large number of studies showing the emergence of children (eighteen to twenty-four months) pretending and also recognizing the pretense of others. By thirty-six to forty-eight months, children understand "knowing" and that it is the product of perception. By this time, they also have begun to recognize false beliefs; that is, they have begun to understand the difference between believing that something is the case and believing that something is the case when it is not the case.

Baron-Cohen also appeals to neurological evidence for his theoretical claims. He asserts that there is evidence that the ID may be localized in the superior temporal sulcus (STS) and that Perret et al. (1991), on the basis of single-cell recording, report that some cells in the STS fire significantly more often when the animal in the test observes an agent doing something. He says that these cells can be regarded as part of the ID because almost any detection of action will involve attributing a goal or desire to an agent (Baron-Cohen 1995: 93). According to Baron-Cohen, Perrett and his co-workers also report having found cells in the same region of the cortex that respond to self-propelled motion, which, as we have already seen, Premack emphasizes is a fundamental property of the attribution of agency.

Other Voices

The psychological news discloses, then, that the requisite cognitive equipment for the representation of agency, namely an ARS, is in place very early on, if not at birth. This does not mean that such notions are necessarily coded in the genome. What is innate and what is meant by "innate" are very complex issues, and we do not intend to resolve them here. It is sufficient for us to acknowledge that a number of scholars are rethinking innateness. For example, connectionists such as Elman et al. argue:

> We are prepared to call many universally recurring patterns of behavior—in languages, for example—innate even though we find them nowhere specified directly in the genome. In this sense, our definition of innateness is undoubtedly broader than the traditional view. We also believe that it is richer and more likely to lead to a clearer understanding of how nature shapes its species. (1996: 46)

No matter what the underlying account of innateness is, what does interest us is that experimental work shows that infants have the ability to represent agents and their actions distinctively and that they do so early in development. For example, infants seem to have the ability to detect conspecifics at a very early age. In fact, Meltzoff and Moore (1977, 1983, 1989, 1992) argue that the ability to recognize faces is present at birth.

As we have already pointed out, Premack (1990) not only asserts that infants have the ability to distinguish self-propelled objects from non-self-propelled things but also argues that they have different expectations concerning the behavior of these two categories of things. For example, infants are not surprised to see a ball move when it is hit by another ball, but they are very surprised when a ball moves by itself. They appear to know that simple objects will move only when they have been contacted by another moving object and that other physical objects such as human beings not only can move themselves but also can get other human beings to move without making direct contact with them. It does not take too long for infants to know that they can get mother to act simply by vocalizing, whereas other things in their environment, which are not agents, move only when they are touched.

Such research shows that young children have command of distinctions between agents and everything else well in advance of being able to articulate such distinctions. This suggests that we are dealing with a form of knowledge that is tacit. How such implicit knowledge is acquired is a fascinating question in its own right and whether connectionists are developing the kinds of strategies for finding interesting answers other than simply attributing such abilities "to the genes" is an exciting avenue of research. Nevertheless, we would be remiss if we did not record that connectionist strategies have demonstrated that some representations are likely the inevitable outcomes of minor variations on general network models of learning. The distinction that such researchers employ is between architectural and substantive innateness. Architectural innateness refers to the way in which neural networks are organized such that they are predisposed to respond to certain kinds of information rapidly and efficiently. Substantive innateness argues for the presence of ideas in the mind at birth because they are the products of a process that originates due to genetic encoding.

To conclude this section, we ought to note that it is possible to be skeptical about our emphasis upon agency generally and on CPS agents in particular. Or to put it another way: even if all of this information about agency is true, what does that have to do with theorizing about religion? One line of attack could focus upon theological thought and argue that within at least some religious traditions, the focus of the religion seems to be notions that transcend agency. For example, some philosophical theologians have developed highly abstract notions such as "Being-itself" as central notions in the conceptual schemes of particular religious traditions. Our potential critics might be tempted to argue that if such theologians were correct, then CPS agents would not deserve the attention that we have afforded them in our theory. Another line of attack could call attention to religious traditions such as Buddhism in which notions such as *nirvana* are central, not agency. Another line of attack, for example, the "God is dead" movement, "secular city," and so on, could point to the attempt of some religious thinkers to focus upon ethical norms rather than agency.

My answer to such possible objections takes two forms. For the sake of argument, I am willing to bite the bullet and argue that I am talking about situations in which groups of individuals seem to share representations about superhuman agents and are mutually involved in a system of practices that are informed by such representations of agency. If our critics do not wish to call such ideas and the practices they inform "religion," we can live with that. Nevertheless, I have proposed a theory that accounts for a widespread set of phenomena found in many different cultures throughout human history.

My second answer involves the significant findings of those scholars such as Stewart Guthrie (1993, and this volume), who have studied the widespread phenomenon of anthropomorphism from an anthropological perspective. Furthermore, there have been important experimental findings (Barrett and Keil 1996; Barrett) that point to a basic human tendency to anthropomorphize not only features of the natural world but also the concept of a superhuman agent itself. We shall discuss both of these approaches later.

The Relevance of This Research for Religious Representations

For our purposes, it suffices to identify the early forms of knowledge that very young children seem to possess and to show the importance of this fact for

PSYCHOLOGICAL PERSPECTIVES ON AGENCY

understanding agency in religious ritual contexts. Because our theory focuses upon the central role that CPS agents play in religious ritual representations, it is open to theoretical and experimental support from those investigations in cognitive psychology that are concerned to discover and elaborate upon core notions such as agency. In our earlier work (1990), we have made the claim that religious representations are dependent upon our ordinary systems for the representation of action. Work in the psychology of agency should, therefore, provide some clues concerning the psychology of religious agency, since the notion of agents with special qualities (only the content of which is defined by conceptual schemes in specific cultural situations) is parasitic upon our ordinary notions of agency.

I shall discuss first how our cognitive equipment is activated by certain stimuli in such a manner that they generate religious representations of CPS agents (Spiro 1966). The first bit of evidence comes from the study of the widespread human predisposition to trade heavily in anthropomorphism. Humans not only have the capacity to detect other human beings at an early age and are able to distinguish them from all other things but also seem to be addicted to seeing human forms even when they are not really there. They have touchy agency detection devices (ADDs). Here, Stewart Guthrie (1993, and this volume) has shown how widespread anthropomorphism is. Humans see faces not only in the clouds but also on the surface of Mars, in abstract patterns, in artifacts, and in just about every conceivable kind of thing. "Faces and other human forms seem to pop out at us on all sides. Chance images in clouds, in landforms, and in ink blots present eyes, profiles, or whole figures. Voices murmur or whisper in wind and waves. We see the world not only as alive but also as humanlike" (Guthrie 1993: 62).

Guthrie also points to the anthropomorphic character of religion:

> People who say religion is anthropomorphism usually mean one of two different things: either that it attributes human characteristics to gods or that, in claiming gods exist, it attributes human characteristics to nature. In the former meaning, religion makes gods human-like at least in crediting them with the capacity for symbolic action. In the latter, which is what I mean, religion makes nature humanlike by seeing gods there. (Guthrie 1993: 177)

From Guthrie's point of view, the fact that religions postulate gods with humanlike qualities is less important than the fact that religious representations depend upon anthropomorphic representations. These representations simply are one way of interpreting the world around us by imposing human properties upon various objects in the environment.

Guthrie has documented the pervasiveness of the human tendency to anthropomorphize. Cross-cultural studies show that anthropomorphism is pervasive and recurrent. But Guthrie is more interested in interpreting what people are doing, that is, describing nature anthropomorphically, than in accounting for such a tendency in cognitive terms. Or to put it another way, Guthrie has not theorized about the cognitive mechanisms involved. He simply assumes that they must exist. One of the points that Guthrie misses is that people do not only anthropomorphize what they see—that is, they do not only attribute agency to various aspects of the natural world—but they also attribute agency to that which is behind the world we see, that is, to the world that is hidden from our senses.

Barrett and Keil (1996) show that even when people possess conventional ideas about the gods, for example, the gods know everything, can be everywhere at once, are all-powerful, and so on, they nevertheless have a tendency to think of the gods in anthropomorphic rather than abstract theological terms. Barrett and Keil have devised experiments to show that even when human beings possess complex theologies and are capable of sophisticated talk about the counterintuitive properties of the CPS agents in such theologies and even when they have lists of concepts applicable only to such entities, for example, omniscience, omnipotence, and omnipresence, nevertheless, when they are required to engage in reasoning about the gods referred to in those theologies, in the midst of larger cognitive tasks, they do not integrate such theologically elaborated formulations into their online reasoning about the gods. Instead, their reasoning relies on more everyday, anthropomorphic conceptions of these agents. Such gods do not know everything, are not omnipotent, and cannot be everywhere at once.

Barrett and Keil examine the representation of non-natural entities such as God by testing their subjects' comprehension of narratives. In one experiment, Barrett and Keil tell the subjects a story about a boy who is swimming alone in a river and becomes entangled in some rocks with no possible means of escape. Fearing that he will drown, he begins to struggle and pray. God is answering another prayer in another part of the world but before long responds to the boy's prayer by pushing one of the rocks so that the boy can free himself. The boy escapes to the bank, exhausted yet free. The subjects, after having heard the story, are asked a series of questions. Their answers reveal that the subjects misremembered the stories in an anthropomorphic way. For example, they remember wrongly that God stops hearing one prayer in order to respond to another. But Barrett and Keil do not speculate about what kind of cognitive mechanism is at work other than to distinguish between online and offline cognitive processing, that is, explicit, reflective, conscious reasoning as opposed to implicit, nonreflective, nonconscious inference.

Pascal Boyer (1994) has furthered the analysis of the role that agency plays in religious thought through his elaboration of the intuitive ontologies that all human beings employ in their common sense reasoning. An intuitive ontology is a "theory" of the kinds of things that there are in the world. It consists of a set of categories containing such notions as persons, animals, plants, physical and artificial objects, and a set of default assumptions about these categories. For example, plants are physical objects that do not have minds but are capable of various biological processes such as growth and death. Being in command of such an ontology automatically makes available to each person sets of inferences that accompany the deployment of the categories. In such an intuitive ontology, human beings, for example, are represented as agents possessing the properties of intentionality, animacy, and physicality. We may call these the default assumptions of the notion of a person. Other categories in these intuitive ontologies are "animal," "plant," "artificial object," and "physical object." Boyer maintains that such notions are part of our standard cognitive equipment and are regularly deployed in our day-to-day cognitive traffic with the world.

Boyer is particularly concerned with the cognitive dynamics of the cultural transmission of religious concepts. He wants to show how such standard cognitive equipment can yield surprising results when the default assumptions of the various categories are violated. Violation of the default assumptions associated with the ontological categories takes two forms, either via a breach of one of the default assumptions of the category in question or a transfer of one of the default assumptions to another category. For example, breaching the assumption that a person has a body, that is, violating the default assumption of a person's physicality yields the representation of a person who has a mind and is alive but has no physical properties. As we all know, many religions contain the notions of angels, spirits, gods, ghosts, and "powers" that can think, plan, punish, and cajole; these entities are very much alive, yet they are disembodied.

Besides breaching the assumptions associated with a category, there is the additional resource of transfer available to generate out-of-the-ordinary or counterintuitive concepts. Transferring properties from one category to another also is available for religious purposes. For example, transferring intentional properties to objects not normally thought to possess them, for example, artifacts, or even naturally occurring objects such as mountains, trees, or animals, yields the sorts of concepts that regularly occur in religious conceptual systems. Attributing the property of intentionality to a statue, for example, generates the concept of a statue that can read our thoughts or deliver secret information to us. Attributing the property of intentionality to a divining board generates the concept of an artificial object that can predict our future.

The discipline of comparative religion has produced volumes about religious conceptual schemes replete with such notions. What Boyer intends to demonstrate is that such counterintuitive notions are memorable and are, therefore, more easily transmitted culturally. But there are definite constraints on transmission. The counterintuitive features of notions that contain violations of the default assumptions of the categories must exemplify a cognitive optimum with the intuitive features, that is, features that are simply taken for granted. Too much violation leads to overkill; too little leads to boredom.

In analyzing our susceptibility to including agents with special qualities in our religious representations, Boyer has noted that, in order to make religious representations memorable, we need a bit of the exotic or counterintuitive thrown in. His notion of the cognitive optimum is interesting because it shows that there is an optimum between schematic and nonschematic ideas that, when reached, makes it more likely that such ideas will be transmitted.

Recently, Boyer (1998) has subjected some of these claims to experimental tests. Boyer devised three studies that employed free recall and questionnaires to test the recurrence of counterintuitive representations in religious concepts across cultures. Recall data generated by the tests supported Boyer's hypothesis that counterintuitive materials are recalled better than standard items and, therefore, may be more easily transmitted, resulting in cultural spread and stability. Perhaps Boyer's most significant finding is that cultural transmission is not simply a function of bizarreness. Instead, particular combinations of categories and properties are required for transmission. It appears that Boyer has shown that not everything odd goes through; "oddness" comes in different forms, only some of which are transmittable.

The early availability of these cognitive resources shows why explicit instruction is not prominent in the acquisition of such notions. Such cognitive resources arise quite naturally in the course of human cognitive development. Representing the world via such processes as violation and transfer comes so easily to us. Our minds are prepared to traffic in agency. Superhuman agency simply adds special qualities to the standard notion of agents with mechanical, teleological, and intentional properties. When we think about the gods as agents capable of acting for our good or ill, our judgments are both constrained and enhanced by our intuitive ontologies. As Barrett and Keil say:

> The problem created by the ontological chasm between humans and the supernatural is solved by ignoring the difference. It appears we accept information about God quite literally. No longer is God a wholly different being, inexplicable and unpredictable. God is understood as a superhuman and likely to behave as we do. The problem is addressed by creating God in the image of ourselves, and using the constraints of nature and humanity as our basic assumptions for understanding God. So it appears that the God of many people is not quite so different from Zeus as it might at first seem. (1996: 244)

Cognitive Evidence for Religious Agency

If it is the case that human beings easily postulate CPS agents and the actions they perform, then we need to determine the features of this susceptibility. It should be clear by now that we think that the susceptibility to religious agency is parasitic on the susceptibility to agency itself. We are capable of thinking of agents with special qualities because we are predisposed to think of agents with ordinary qualities. A number of cognitive scientists provide expert guidance on this matter. Frank Keil (1979) argues that in normal conceptual development, human beings who normally avoid predicate spanning, that is, applying predicates applicable to one ontological category to another, have no qualms under certain conditions about extending features that are characteristic of one category to another. For example, normally we know that if something is made of metal, such as a watch, then we would not predicate the ability to breathe to it. So, if someone says, "My watch is snoring," we either think they have made a category mistake or that they are making a metaphorical statement meaning, for example, that the watch is ticking very loudly. The point is that we know it if people are engaging in the act of predicate spanning. When we engage in predicate spanning, we find ourselves in the world of metaphor and myth. In fact, focusing upon "breaking the rules" of predicate attribution opens the windows of cognition to the contents of the conceptual schemes of humankind's religions.

As we already have seen in the work of Boyer, religious ideas are filled with the notions of persons without bodies, beings who live forever, animals that predict the future, statues that record and transmit information, and so on. Perhaps what is most intriguing is that such cognitive activities are not only widely distributed in space and time, but they also seem to start at a very young age in every generation, often to the despair of atheistic parents bothered by the gullibility of their children.

The predisposition to employ the concept of religious agency also can be understood by looking at work in social psychology. Attribution theorists have mounted evidence concerning the role that agency plays in human judgment. In fact, it seems to be the case that human beings have the propensity to overextend attributions of agency even when the situation does not require such attribution (Ross 1977). What is involved here is not so much the error of overattribution as it is the preoccupation that humans seem to have with agent causality. Conspiracy theories abound. Blame is placed even when it is not required. Human beings' preoccupation with agent causality typically results in their underestimation of the role of the environment and their overestimation of human responsibility and the role of personality traits when assessing the causal dynamics of social events. When the chips are down, it seems to be easier and more efficient to credit human agency in making social judgments than it is to find underlying causes. The process of identifying hidden causes is far more difficult and far more costly for humans generally (McCauley 1998).

Historians and philosophers of science who are concerned to specify what is involved in the growth of knowledge also have paid attention to the notion of agency and specifically to how religious agency has often, in fact, frustrated the development of scientific theorizing. Paul Churchland (1989) argues that as our knowledge of the world increases, attributions of agency retreat. But he also acknowledges that attributions of agency have played an important role in folk psychology throughout human history.

Of course, while it may be true that scientifically minded people are slowly beginning to abandon the range of the application of agency, it is not at all obvious that it is true of our online mode of reasoning, as Barrett and Keil have demonstrated. Reasoning in terms of agency is efficient in dealing with the world, and the appeal to superhuman agents is a powerful strategy in explaining unexpected results. Operating theaters are filled with claims of miracles! Whatever forces may contribute to such representations of agency, human cultures are pervaded by them, and they seem to spread by contagion. Anything that spreads so easily needs to be accounted for.

How then do the various types of information referred to above fit with our theory of religious ritual? We have argued that religious ritual participants possess a system of implicit knowledge by means of which they make judgments about ritual form. They make judgments not only based upon the Principle of Superhuman Agency (henceforth PSA) but also on the basis of the Principle of Superhuman Immediacy (henceforth PSI). The PSA requires that superhuman agents must be represented somewhere in the system of ritual representation. The PSI requires that where in the system the agents appear makes all the difference about the kinds of judgments that religious participants will make. Not only are religious participants capable of detecting agents (agency detection device [ADD]), but they also are capable of attributing the special qualities that such agents must possess in order to be efficacious.

For example, religious participants seem to know that in order to become initiated into the sacred traditions of the group, they must be subject to the actions performed by agents in order for the initiation to prove efficacious. But they also seem to know that these agents must possess special qualities for them to accomplish the jobs they need to accomplish. In a particular case, these agents may be the elders, but these elders may perform the initiation rites only because they, in turn, have been initiated by an earlier set of elders who were initiated. This explains the advent of superhuman agents, since the buck stops with the gods. The system of implicit knowledge with which religious participants operate in particular situations makes available to them a set of inferences about who is qualified to perform what rite, what agents must be present in order for the rite to be performed, what actions must be performed in order for the rite to be successful, what agents must perform the rite, what qualifies one to be a patient in such a situation, what distinguishes a successful action from an unsuccessful one, and so on. The cognitive mechanisms in place enable ritual participants to know the difference between an agent, an action, and a patient and to know the means by which the action is performed. Ritual participants also know implicitly the special qualities that agents and/or patients should possess in order for the ritual to accomplish its objectives.

Such predictions about the judgments that religious participants will make about ritual form raise empirical questions. In recent work, Barrett and Lawson (in press) have designed a set of experiments to test three empirical predictions: (I) individuals unfamiliar with a particular ritual, religious system still will have converging intuitions about whether or not a particular ritual is well formed; (2) ritually naïve individuals still will appreciate the central importance of superhuman agency being represented somewhere in the ritual structure; and (3) subjects will judge having an appropriate agent for a given ritual most important to the success or failure of a ritual action.

The experiments by Barrett and Lawson directly tapped participants' intuitions regarding ritual structures by presenting fictitious rituals that were deemed well formed (because they were successful), altering these rituals, and then asking for relative judgments about what changes in the ritual would most likely undermine their effectiveness. The subjects were sixty-eight students recruited from introductory psychology courses at a Protestant college in the United States. They ranged in age from 17 to 22 years old, with a mean age of 18.6 years. Forty were female and twenty-eight were male. A packet of twelve randomly ordered ritual sets was prepared. A prototype ritual was followed by twelve variations including a reproduction of the prototype. An example of a prototype ritual was, "A special person blew ordinary dust on a field and the field yielded good crops." The twelve variations of the prototype included (1) a version of the prototype with S markers (references to agents with special qualities) in both the agent and instrument slots, for example, "A special person blew special dust on a field and the field yielded good crops," (2) a version with an S marker only in the agent slot, (3) a version with an S marker only in the instrument slot, (4) a version with no S markers but otherwise identical to the prototype, (5) a minor agent change (to an animal) with an S marker, (6) a minor agent change with no S marker, (7) a major agent change to (to an inanimate object) with an S marker, (8) a major change without an S marker, (9 and 10) two action changes otherwise identical to the prototype, (11) an instrument change with an S marker, and (12) an instrument change without an S marker. Participants were asked to rate on 7-point scales how likely each of the changes was to account for the failure of the second ritual, that is, which changes were important in undermining the effectiveness of the ritual. A low score meant that it was extremely likely that the ritual would work, and 7 meant that it was extremely unlikely for the ritual to be effective.

The results of the experiment were encouraging. As predicted, the two marker items (items marked by the presence of agents with special qualities) were rated significantly lower than the other marker items. (M[Median] = 2.00 compared to the next closest type of marker item.) The two S-marker items even differed significantly from the no-marker items when the prototype had no S markers and so the no-marker choices best approximated the successful actions. The two forms of one-marker items did not differ significantly from each other but had significantly lower average ratings than the no-marker items (M = 3.06 for the S marker in the instrument slot; M = 4.65 for the no-marker items.) The two one-marker types did not differ significantly from the no-marker items when the prototype had no S marker. It seems S markers do matter to subjects' judgment of the well-formedness, and therefore the effectiveness, of rituals even if S markers are not necessarily included in the prototype rituals.

The second prediction regarding S markers was that not having S markers would damage the rituals' likelihood of success, more so than other changes such as action and instrument. Since some of the prototype rituals did not have S markers, testing this hypothesis is muddied. By implicitly being told one-quarter of the time that markers are unnecessary, subjects may have devalued S markers relative to other features. More importantly, in cases when the prototype had no S markers, the no S-marker item does not constitute the removal of S markers but is a reiteration of the ritual that supposedly worked. To minimize these difficulties, the measure chosen to represent the importance of S markers in the ritual structure relative to other components was the average of no S-marker items only in cases when the prototype had at least one S marker. In these cases, the no S-marker condition truly indicated the removal or absence of an S marker. As predicted, this "S-marker absent" score was greater than either the action or instrument scores. The mean "S-marker absent" score was 5.26 as compared with 3.60 for action changes, and 4.39 for instrument changes. Subjects' intuitions even converged on agent changes being less important for ritual success than the presence of S markers. Agent change items had a mean rating of 4.71.

Consistent with the predictions regarding agents, agent changes with and without S markers were rated as more damaging to the possible success of the rituals than action changes. Agent changes with an S marker ("special" agents) had a mean rating of 4.29, which was significantly different from instrument changes. Agent changes without an S marker were judged as even more likely to ruin the rituals (M = 5.i2) and were rated significantly different from both action changes and instrument changes.

Subjects' ratings indicated that if a ritual gives no indication that the agent or instrument involved has been endowed with special properties or authority by a divine source (removing S markers), then it will not bring about the desired non-natural consequences. The representation of agents with special qualities somewhere in ritual structure was judged as more important for the success of the ritual than using the original instrument of performing the proper action. Subjects' ratings also suggest intuitions that more than one indication of superhuman agency in the action structure is better than only one. Finally, in these religious actions, subjects' intuitions were that having an agent capable of intending a particular outcome was more important than performing a particular action. Changing an action was not as devastating to the intended consequence even if the agent was performing the appropriate action.

To sum up, the results of the experiment confirmed the first prediction by showing that two S markers were better than one and that one was better than none. They also confirmed the second prediction by showing that not having S markers would more likely damage the efficacy of an action than either action or instrument changes. And the results confirmed the third prediction that changes in the agent slot were more damaging than changes in any other aspect of the ritual structure.

These two experiments were designed to test three general predictions in Lawson and McCauley (1990): (1) that people have converging intuitions about the efficacy, that is, well-formedness, of rituals; (2) that when judging the efficacy of a ritual, superhuman agency will be more important than any other aspect of ritual; and (3) that people will regard having an appropriate agent as relatively more important than the particular action involved. The strategy employed by Barrett and Lawson to test these predictions involved tapping people's intuitions by presenting them with fictitious rituals identified as effective, altering their form in specific ways, and then asking the subjects to make relative judgments about what kind of changes in the presented rituals would most likely undermine their effectiveness. The results of the experiments supported all three predictions.

Rather than guessing at random, which would have produced mean ratings around the midpoint of the scales, the subjects, who were unfamiliar with the fictitious rituals, seemed to possess converging intuitions about what in the ritual structure was most important for each ritual's success. The subjects also seemed to understand that for an action to produce special consequences, superhuman agency must be involved in some way and that a connection with superhuman agents is the best predictor of success. Rather than simply rating the rituals that best matched the prototype as most likely to be effective and ignoring the importance of S markers, the subjects recognized the importance of superhuman agency. They favored ritual forms with "special" agents or "special" instruments when "specialness" was defined as having been endowed with unusual properties from the gods. And, finally, participants' intuitions converged on the point that having an appropriate agent for a ritual is relatively more important than the specific action involved. Having an agent that does more than merely perform the action but also intends the consequences of the action is more important than the actions themselves in determining the efficacy of the action involved.

A theory about religious ritual intuitions, then, is empirically tractable and capable of being tested to highlight the role that ritual intuitions with noncultural foundations play in making religious ritual judgments. This means that a cognitive psychology of religion may begin to demonstrate that, in order to connect the cognitive and the cultural, it is worth focusing upon the noncultural foundations of religious ideas and the practices they inform.

References

Barkow, J., J. Tooby, and L. Cosmides (1992). *The Adapted Mind*, Oxford: Oxford University Press.

Baron-Cohen, S. (1995). *Mindblindness: An Essay on Autism and Theory of Mind*, Cambridge, MA: The MIT Press.

Baron-Cohen, S., and J. Swettenham (1996). "The Relationship Between SAM and ToMM: Two Hypotheses," in *Theories of Mind*, edited by P. Carruthers and P. K. Smith, 158–68, Cambridge: Cambridge University Press.

Barrett, J. L., and F. C. Keil (1996). "Conceptualizing a Non-Natural Entity: Anthropomorphism in God Concepts," *Cognitive Psychology* 31: 219–47.

Barrett, J. L., and E. T. Lawson (Forthcoming). "Ritual Intuitions: Cognitive Contributions to Judgments of Ritual Efficacy," *Journal of Cognition and Culture*.

Boyer, P. (1994). *The Naturalness of Religious Ideas: A Cognitive Theory of Religion*, Oakland CA: University of California Press.

Boyer, P. (1998). "Cognitive Tracks of Cultural Inheritance: How Evolved Intuitive Ontology Governs Cultural Transmission," *American Anthropologist* 100 (4): 876–89.

Butterworth, G. (1991). "The Ontogeny and Phylogeny of Joint Visual Attention," in *Natural Theories of Mind: Evolution, Development, and Simulation*, edited by A. Whiten, 223–32, Oxford: Blackwell.

Carruthers, P., and P. K. Smith, eds. (1996). *Theories of Theories of Mind*, Cambridge: Cambridge University Press.

Churchland, P. (1989). *A Neurocomputational Perspective: The Nature of Mind and The Structure of Science*, Cambridge, MA: The MIT Press.

Dennett, D. C. (1987). *The Intentional Stance*, Cambridge, MA: The MIT Press.

Elman, J. (1996). *Rethinking Innateness: A Connectionist Perspective on Development*, Cambridge, MA: The MIT Press.

Fodor. (1983). *The Modularity of Mind*, Cambridge, MA: The MIT Press.

Guthrie, S. (1993). *Faces in the Clouds*, New York: Oxford University Press.
Heider, F., and M. Simmel (1944). "An Experimental Study of Apparent Behavior," *American Journal of Psychology* 57: 243–59.
Hietanen, J., and D. Perret (1991). "A Role of Expectation in Visual and Tactile Processing Within the Temporal Cortex," in *Brain Mechanisms of Perception and Memory: From Neuron to Behavior*, edited by T. Ono, M. Fukuda, L. R. Squire, M. E. Raichle, and D. L. Perrett, 83–103, Oxford: Oxford University Press.
Keil, F. C. (1979). *Semantic and Conceptual Development*, Cambridge, MA: The MIT Press.
Lawson, E. T., and R. N. McCauley (1990). *Rethinking Religion: Connecting Cognition and Culture*, Cambridge: Cambridge University Press.
Leslie, A. M. (1982). "The Perception of Causality in Infants," *Perception* 11: 173–86.
Leslie, A. M. (1984). "Infant Perception of a Manual Pickup Event," *British Journal of Developmental Psychology* 2: 19–32.
Leslie, A. M. (1996 [1995]). "A Theory of Agency," in *Causal Cognition: A Multidisciplinary Debate*, edited by D. Sperber, D. Premack, and A. J. Premack, 121–47, New York: Oxford University Press.
Leslie, A. M., and S. Keeble (1987). "Do Six-Month-Old Infants Perceive Causality?" *Cognition* 25: 265–88.
Maurer D., and M. E. Barrera (1981). "The Perception of Facial Expression by the Three-Month-Old," *Child Development* 52 (1): 203–6.
McCauley, R. N. (1998). "Comparing the Cognitive Foundations of Religion and Science," Emory Cognition Project, Report no. 37, September 1998, Department of Psychology, Emory University, Atlanta, GA.
Meltzoff, A. N., and M. K. Moore (1977). "Imitation of Facial and Manual Gestures by Human Neonates," *Science* 198: 75–8.
Meltzoff, A. N., and M. K. Moore (1983). "Newborn Infants Imitate Adult Facial Gestures," *Child Development* 54: 702–9.
Meltzoff, A. N., and M. K. Moore (1989). "Imitation in New-Born Infants: Exploring the Range of Gestures Imitated and the Underlying Mechanisms," *Developmental Psychology* 25: 954–62.
Meltzoff, A. N., and M. K. Moore (1992). "Early Imitation within a Functional Framework: The Importance of Person Identity, Movement, and Development," *Infant Behavior and Development* 15: 479–505.
Meltzoff, A. N., and M. K. Moore (1994). "Imitation, Memory, and the Representation of Persons," *Infant Behavior and Development* 17: 83–99.
Michotte, A. (1963). *The Perception of Causality*, Andover: Methuen.
Mithen, S. (1996). The Prehistory of the Mind: The Cognitive Origins of Art, Religion and Science, New York: Thames and Hudson.
Perret, D., M. Hietanen, W. Oram, and P. Benson (1991). "Organization and Function of Cells Responsive to Faces in the Temporal Cortex," *Philosophical Transactions of the Royal Society of London, B* 223: 293–317.
Perret, D., and A. Mistlin (1990). "Perception of Facial Characteristics by Monkeys," in *Comparative Perception, Volume 2: Complex Signals*, edited by W. Stebbins and M. Berkely, 187–215, New York: Wiley.
Premack, D. (1990). "Infant's Theory of Self-Propelled Objects," *Cognition* 36: 1–16.

Reddy, V. (1991). "Playing with Other's Expectations: Teasing and Mucking About in the First Year," in *Natural Theories of Mind: Evolution, Development and Simulation of Everyday Mindreading*, edited by A. Whiten, 143–58, Oxford: Blackwell.

Ross, L. D. (1977). "The Intuitive Psychologist and His Shortcomings: Distortions in the Attribution Process," in *Advances in Experimental Social Psychology*, vol. x, edited by L. Berkowitz, 173–220, New York: Random House.

Scaife, M., and J. Bruner (1975). "The Capacity of Joint Attention in the Infant," *Mature* 253: 256–66.

Spelke, E. (1991). "Physical Knowledge in Infancy: Reflections on Piaget's Theory," in *The Epigenesis of Mind: Essays in Biology and Cognition*, edited by S. Carey and R. Gelman, 133–69, Hillsdale: Erlbaum.

Spelke, E., A. Phillips, and A. L Woodward (1996 [1995]). "Infant's Knowledge of Object Motion and Human Action," in *Causal Cognition: A Multidisciplinary Debate*, edited by D. Sperber, D. Premack, and A. J. Premack, 44–78, New York: Oxford University Press.

Sperber, D. (1975). *Rethinking Symbolism*, Cambridge: Cambridge University Press.

Sperber, D. (1990). "The Epidemiology of Beliefs," in *The Social Psychological Study of Widespread Belief*, edited by C. Eraser and G. Gaskel, 25–44, Oxford: Clarendon Press.

Sperber, D. (1996). *Explaining Culture*, Cambridge, MA: Blackwell.

Spiro, M. (1966). "Religion: Problems of Definition and Meaning," in *Anthropological Approaches to the Study of Religion*, edited by M. Banton, 85–126, London: Tavistock.

Warrington, E., and T. Shalice (1984). "Category Specific Semantic Impairments," *Brain* 107: 829–54.

INTRODUCTION TO CHAPTER 9

The aim of this chapter is to suggest that it is worthwhile seeing what the various studies in the cognitive science of religion have taught us about "religion" by engaging in a thought experiment in which we ask: "What would it take to create a religion on the basis of what we think that we now know about religiosity?" It will be an exercise in applied science by following a set of instructions and I hope will also be a lot of fun. I tried this out on my students in Brno, the Czech Republic, and received a very good response.

9

How to Create a Religion

There can no longer be any doubt that the cognitive (and evolutionary) science of religion, CSR, is a vibrant and progressive research program with participants from a wide range of disciplines and from many parts of the world. Theoretical, empirical, and experimental work proceeds apace. Many issues are being addressed in conferences, books, and scientific journals. Some of the most interesting have been projects focused upon issues such as (1) whether particular religious notions are by-products or adaptations, (2) the distinction between theological correctness and intuitive notions, (3) the role that counterintuitive notions play in cultural transmission, (4) the importance of notions of biological and psychological death and the role such notions play in afterlife beliefs, (5) credibility enhancing displays, (6) the utility of the distinction between transmitted and evoked culture, (7) costly signaling, and (8) the role that "Big Gods" play in the evolution of religious systems and so on. Some of this work has been examined carefully in books such as Martin and Wiebe's *Religion Explained? The Cognitive Science of Religion after Twenty-five Years.*[1] The aim of this chapter is to suggest that it is worthwhile seeing what these studies have taught us by engaging in a thought experiment in which we ask: "What would it take to create a religion on the basis of what we think that we now know about religiosity?"

I was inspired to attempt this task after having read Richard P. Feynman's *Six Easy Pieces: Essentials of Physics Explained*,[2] a work in which he throws out the following challenge: "If you can't build it you don't understand it!"

Let us, therefore, imagine a situation in which I am asked the question, "So, what instructions would you give a person who wishes to consciously create a religion that at least has some chance of succeeding?"

First, I would argue that you need something for people to think about. This means that you will need a set of ideas set within the framework of a story. Let us call this framework the conceptual scheme. This conceptual scheme should consist of a set of agents as well as narratives, oral or written, that will play a specific part in the actions that the agents are engaged in and also a set of one or more experiences which involves some change in status as a consequence of the actions of the agents. At least one of the agents in the conceptual scheme will have to possess some minimally counterintuitive qualities that will set this agent apart from all of the other agents described by the conceptual scheme.

The second requirement in this creative process is that the agents in the story need something to think about but also something to do. Let us, therefore, prescribe a set of actions that have some relation to the set of ideas in the conceptual scheme. Let us call this the "action-representation system." This system will have a very simple structure: somebody does something to someone by means of an instrument of some kind. This structure should not be confused with another structure; that is, somebody does something. What is the difference? Well, you can do something without doing something *to* somebody! You can, for example, whistle, laugh, sing, pray, dance, or just think without such actions being done to somebody or something. We will find out, in due course, why this is an important distinction but at this point let me just say that religiosity can involve actions that do not bring about a change in status. On the other hand, some of the most important actions in any religion do so whether we are talking about what Whitehouse[3] has called imagistic and doctrinal religions. We have here two structures to employ in our creation of a religion. In one case we have an agent doing something such as chanting, (agent-action) and in the other an agent doing something to someone or something by means of an instrument (agent-action-patient-instrument), such as when an agent touches a patient (the recipient of the action) with a stick.

In the first case, chanting is something, in this particular religious context, which one typically does in particular situations, for example, at various points in a religious service. In the second case being touched by a stick would

HOW TO CREATE A RELIGION

signify that the recipient of the action has a new status "having been touched by a stick." (Think, for example, of someone having been knighted by the queen by means of being touched by a sword.)

But now we also begin to see why you should expect there to be at least one agent that needs a special (counterintuitive) quality because not just anybody can bring about a change of status simply by touching someone else by an instrument of some kind. The agent must be qualified to bring about the change, and I suppose the instrument had better be qualified as well. In a particular system of knighthood, only the regent can confer knighthood.

How does the qualification come about? I can think of three ways: by inheritance. "I am qualified to bring about the change of status because I inherited the quality from my ancestors." Or I can do so by being made qualified by a person already qualified who makes me qualified by means of a special action involving an instrument of some kind. "I was touched by an instrument with special qualities which was made special by an agent with special qualities" or by a special experience which my followers are willing to attribute to me or credit me as having. "I experienced a special feeling unlike any other kind of feeling and that makes it possible for me to bring about a change of status in someone else." I am sure the reader can easily find illustrations of all three forms of "qualification" in particular religious traditions, ethnographic reports, or historical accounts of religious practices. In any case, in the religion we are creating, qualification is an important component in the conceptual scheme and in the action-representation system.

Having established the structure of the action that distinguishes between kinds of actions and having highlighted those that bring about some kind of change of status, it is important to recognize that these sets of actions will have to be *connected to one another* in quite specific ways. Let us take an easy example. In order to become a member of a particular religion one has to undergo the act of being initiated into the community either by being, for example, immersed in water or being sprinkled by water. As we have already seen, the agent performing the initiation must be qualified to do so. In order to be qualified, the agent performing the initiation has to have already been initiated. In this religion, initiation is a necessary condition for being able to initiate someone. It is not, however, a *sufficient* condition because the agent will also have to have been initiated in order to be initiated, which is another special set of actions. In fact, that process or chain of actions is only conceived of as having been stopped by the originator of the entire process, a CI agent! So in creating a religion one would have to have an entry "ritual" or set of actions and one or more sets of qualification actions to make the whole system work. You most probably will also need to have a "leaving" or even an "expulsion" ritual.

There is, however, much more to do. One will find that while some actions will be done frequently, others will only be done occasionally. If you only have one ritual, then frequent repetition will lead to boredom. So you had better have more than one. In fact, it might make sense to have two kinds of rituals, the first kind to do frequently to keep one focused and identified with the community and the second one to be done infrequently so that it can be seen as being a special event. Underlying this requirement is the idea that it is important to make some of the actions in this religion memorable and worth celebrating or at least distinguishing them from all of the other actions in the religion. The most memorable ones are those that are only done once; the least memorable, because they are almost automatic, are those done most frequently. Now let us connect the most memorable ones with the CI agent either directly or indirectly performing the set of actions upon the initiate, whereas the most frequent ones have the initiate performing the set of actions upon the CI agent. In the first case, the CI agent does the action either directly or through an intermediary, while in the second, the receiver of the action, the patient, does the action to the CI agent. In our design, I would argue that it is better to have both kinds rather than just one or the other, that is, unique versus repetitive rituals. If you only have a unique ritual then there is something to look back upon, there is nothing to look forward to, whereas if you only have repetitive actions there is nothing to look either back to or forward to because it is simply boring, "the same old same old!" Unique events grab our attention and repetitive acts lead to habituation. What we see in these two kinds of rituals is that unique rituals focus upon the qualities of the agent, the initiator of the action, whereas in the repetitive rituals, the focus is on the qualities of the recipient. The best way to achieve memorability and, therefore, the persistence of our religion is to enhance memorability by raising the emotions. And the best way to raise the emotions is by encouraging sensory pageantry. So in our religion we will have occasional festivals, powerful initiations, and day-to-day simple acts to remind us that we belong to a religion.

Apart from the qualities of the initiator and the initiated, it is also worth specifying the actions themselves especially when those actions themselves should have an extraordinary property that distinguishes them from ordinary actions, for example, washing oneself when one is already clean, wearing special clothes when one already has sufficient clothing, butchering an animal not for eating but for classifying relationships, and so on. This is known as goal demotion where the typical purpose is distinguishable from its ritual purpose (Boyer and Lienard 2006). The ritual purpose can be explicit, that is to say, the conceptual scheme can give the ritual scenario specific content. That kind of knowledge is usually the consequence of conscious reflection. It is the kind of knowledge that the participants will suggest if questioned about what and why they are doing such things. But it is not the only reason. There might very

HOW TO CREATE A RELIGION

well be a much deeper and unconscious reason why people are motivated to perform certain kinds of puzzling actions. They feel the necessity to do them but do not really know why. So you can get answers like: we do it because it is the custom, or we do it because other people do it, or don't ask me, ask that person instead. It is worthwhile, therefore, to examine the conditions under which such acts are performed. And this is where evolutionary psychology provides us with important clues. All organisms, and certainly all humans, face situations when they are faced with threats to well-being, for example, predation and assault, contagion, loss of status, and diminution of resources.[4] Such anxiety-causing threats can be immediate or potential. Responses to immediate threats create fear and the typical responses are freezing, fleeing, or fighting. But what we have learned from precautionary psychology[5] is that humans are also attuned to potential threats. Such a capacity leads to devising strategies to attempt to ensure safety. I would expect humans to develop forms of behavior (rituals) to reflect such concerns. In the case of predation and assault, I would expect rituals to reflect strategies that suggest ways to find power to avoid predation and resist assault. In the case of contagion and pollution, I would expect rituals to reflect the notion of prevention, for example, by ritual washing or ingesting palliative substances or acts of cleansing caused by pollution. In the case of loss of status, I would expect the establishing of new forms of status by ritual means. And in the case of loss of resources, I would expect rituals in which a loss of one sort is replaced by gaining resources of a different kind (maybe symbolic?). It certainly is the case when looking at actual rituals how we end up finding the very themes that we would expect to find in rituals. Themes that echo the threats and the solution to threats, for example, ritual washing when already clean.[6]

It will also be important to weigh the costs and benefits of the new religion. In the real world, an action has costs. This is just as true in a religious world because religious notions employ the same ordinary cognitive processes.[7] In light of the various requirements listed earlier, it is clear that costs in time, energy, assets, and establishing social relationships will be present. But there will also be benefits that contribute to fitness, namely, modes of signaling commitment to the religious system, the means of showing group identity, and clear markers of out-group delineation.

If we want this religion to succeed, it will also be important for it to be balanced.[8] Balance involves a number of factors. Dissension in a religion, even a newly created one, is inevitable. An important way to overcome dissension is by achieving conceptual control. Maintaining complexity tends to ensure conceptual control over the system. Conceptual control can be maintained by (1) instituting a hierarchy with entry into any particular level only under special conditions, (2) distinguishing between ritual practitioners and ritual participants, (3) ensuring that the practitioners have a special status (e.g., a priest), (4) requiring the acquisition of special status by means of ritual transition as a patient (i.e., as the recipient of the action), (5) distinguishing between insiders and outsiders and permitting outsiders limited means of participation, and (6) having both frequent and infrequent rituals.

The history of religions shows dissension can never be eliminated but it can and has been controlled. While charismatic figures will play an important role in a developing religion, the balance of the system itself is as important as the originating charismatic figure. In fact, some charismatic figures are very short lived because they failed to intuit the importance of a balanced system. The path to creating a new religion is littered with the bones of charismatic figures who were unable to overcome their own narcissism.

Here my thought experiment ends. I am certain that what I have presented is not the only way that an actual religion, whether imagistic or doctrinal (to use Whitehouse's terms), is formed over time, but I do think that it provides a kind of template or heuristic by means of which we can examine the kinds of data that historians and ethnographers provide us with in their hard work. These researchers are constantly encountering examples of strange substances or even acts regarded as "polluting," odd practices such as shunning or demanding a change of status of someone hierarchically higher, or attitudes to outsiders as infidels, heathens, or sinners. What I have tried to show is that such acts, practices, or attitudes should be expected in the scientific adventure involved in the attempt to explain various forms of human behavior.

Notes

1 Martin and Wiebe (2017).

2 Feynman (1994).

3 Whitehouse (2004).

4 Boyer and Lienard (2006).

5 Szechtman and Woody (2004).

6 Lienard and Lawson (2008).

7 Lawson and McCauley (1990).

8 McCauley and Lawson (2002).

Bibliography

Boyer, P., and P. Lienard (2006). "Why Ritualized Behavior? Precaution Systems and Action Parsing in Developmental, Pathological and Cultural Rituals?" *Behavioral and Brain Sciences* 29 (6): 595–650.

Feynman, R. (1994). *Six Easy Pieces: Essentials of Physics Explained by Its Most Brilliant Teacher*, New York: Perseus Books.

Lawson, E. T., and R. N. McCauley (1990). *Rethinking Religion: Connecting Cognition and Culture*, Cambridge: Cambridge University Press.

Lienard, P., and E. T. Lawson (2008). "Evoked Culture, Ritualization and Religious Rituals," *Religion* 38 (20): 157–71.

Martin, L., and D. Wiebe (2017). *Religion Explained? The Cognitive Science of Religion After Twenty-Five Years*, London and New York: Bloomsbury Publishing.

McCauley, R. N., and E. T. Lawson (2002). *Bringing Ritual to Mind: Psychological Foundations of Cultural Forms*, Cambridge: Cambridge University Press.

Szechtman, H., and E. Woody (2004). "Obsessive Compulsive Disorder as a Disturbance of the Security Motivation System," *Psychological Review* 111 (1): 111–27.

Whitehouse, H. (2004). *Modes of Religiosity: A Cognitive Theory of Religious Transmission*, Oxford: Altamira Press.

PART III

Cognition, Culture, and History

INTRODUCTION TO CHAPTER 10

The study of history seems to be a long way from the scientific study of planets, plants, populations, or paranoias, but all sciences possess a historical aspect. This chapter is an attempt to inspire an interdisciplinary conversation about why that is the case and to encourage consilience. I cannot imagine a full account of religious thought and behavior that ignores the study of human history.

10

History in Science

It has been said more than once that the past is gone for good and that the cognitive science of religion, at least in its experimental garb, is of little help in illuminating us about past religious thought and behavior because the subjects under consideration are dead. We are given a friendly reminder that we are anchored firmly in the present. At most, we receive gracious permission to speculate. While there is some wisdom in this claim, I aim to show that the problems of studying the past experimentally are not insurmountable and, if pursued with dedication and integrity, promise interesting and even important knowledge.

All experiments start with a problem that calls for a solution, a hypothesis to test, a protocol or procedure to test the hypothesis, and a knowledge of statistics to evaluate the results. I will look at five disciplines that are relevant to the issue of studying the past. History, the study of information from the past, primarily texts; archaeology, the study of artifacts from previous eras; evolutionary biology, the study of adaptations built in the past but relevant for the emergence of subsequent organisms; paleontology and geology, the study of the history of the earth as well as its interred inhabitants; and astrophysics and cosmology, the study of the very distant past including the origins of the universe. The light that strikes our eyes now from that shiny object in the sky may have begun its journey billions of years ago.

These disciplines, to a greater or lesser extent, employ rigorous and well-understood scientific methods. Even historians solidly in the humanities tradition have no qualms about appealing to carbon dating to estimate the date of found treasures such as the Dead Sea Scrolls or the Shroud of Turin especially when the claims made about such artifacts are ideologically motivated.

These disciplines understand the difference between interpreting a fact and explaining one. To interpret something is to decide what kind of information to take into consideration when evaluating the significance of an event with the full knowledge that such a decision constrains the choices we make down the line as well as the methods we employ to determine the results. To explain something is to develop an understanding by employing standard techniques that show why it occurred and how the processes worked that brought it about. It is satisfied when it has identified the mechanisms involved.

Let us start with cosmology. Astrophysicists and, in fact, theoretical physicists, generally, have done many interesting things. For example, they succeeded in measuring the speed of light. With that accomplishment in hand, all sorts of other modes of investigation became available, which led to many new theories and ultimately new hypotheses about space and time including the fact that they are inseparable. One consequence that followed was the theory of special relativity, which led to the theory of general relativity later confirmed by experimental work. Recently, scientists have devised experimental procedures to detect gravity waves with some success confirming some of Einstein's theoretical claims. The point here is that rather than the universe being a static nontemporal system, it is historical through and through. Even the laws of physics have a history.

Geology and paleontology also contain a built-in historical element. Geology studies the structure of the earth and in order to understand that structure we need to learn its history. Plate tectonics, when first proposed, was rejected as a fable but now stands as just one shining example of a very successful geological explanation of why we have mountains, why animals are dispersed the way they are, why the continents seem to fit together, and why we have earthquakes. Knowing where in a geological stratum a finding of a set of bones occurs leads to an accurate dating of the time the object found lived and even how it died. Paleontologists have painstakingly unearthed earlier forms of life that are astonishing in their differences from present forms. But note also how paleontology aided by both astrophysical knowledge (meteors and comets) and chemical knowledge (chemical

HISTORY IN SCIENCE

deposited by great impacts) can explain major extinction events such as the demise of the dinosaurs.

Archaeology focuses primarily on human artifacts from the past and the conditions surrounding those artifacts. It explains the conditions capable of bringing about the artifact under consideration, which leads to interpreting its significance in relation to a wider context and subsequent events. Important methods employed to determine accurate dating are radiocarbon dating and thermoluminescence. McCauley and I have already shown how cognitive science in general and cognitive science of religion contribute to interpreting and explaining artifacts from the past (McCauley and Lawson 2007), so I will not repeat the arguments here, but I am convinced that cognitive archaeologists are making great progress in illuminating past events and the minds involved in them. For example, the discovery of a tool tells us not only about the mind that created it but also about the mind that recognizes its use and, perhaps, at a certain point, extends its use in a new direction (Mithen 1996).

But let us return to the environs of the historian and examine a specific case, the discovery of the Qumran texts. Let us look, however, at this from an experimental point of view but told as a fable. Here is a lone historian sitting in her study surrounded by hundreds of volumes all of which she has read and most of which she remembers and a few of which she admires. She is dedicated to studying the past and understanding the forms of behavior that led to certain events that are regarded as very significant in the development of Western civilization. She has a suspicion slowly transforming into a hypothesis that at a certain time and place in history, there were many claimants to the title Messiah. In fact, she expected (hypothesized and retrodicted) that if additional texts were ever to be found from this period there would not only be more texts with stories about Messiahs but that these texts would throw new light on the texts that we already have. Furthermore, she expected that many of the ideas being spread at the time would have much in common with each other. This she based on her presumptions of how minds worked in certain situations. And then, astoundingly, her conjecture was confirmed with the discovery of the Qumran texts. Of course, the way I have structured this story is not the way it happened, but the point I wish to make is that historians, given background knowledge of the past already confirmed, given psychological knowledge of how human minds work in religious situations, and given sociological knowledge of how people perform in groups, can develop hypotheses that predict new knowledge, which can be confirmed or disconfirmed on the basis of new discoveries. Historians can tell us what to look for if we want to understand why and how an event occurred and what we can hope to find if someone left a record somewhere. Before the Qumran texts were discovered, there were already conjectures or hypotheses about what would be the case if certain kinds of texts were found. This is often where the historian can turn to the archaeologist to suggest what to look for, once again demonstrating the interrelatedness of the disciplines.

So, historians traffic in theories which lead to hypotheses (often retrodictions), waiting on discoveries or searching for them, which if successful either confirm or disconfirm the hypotheses, all of which is subject to the rigors of statistical analyses. The trouble is that some historians are simply content to engage in the interpretive task of connecting known facts in new ways.

We might as well also look at the texts that provide the data for historical analysis. What kind of information do they contain? Do they have moral injunctions? If they do, are there good reasons to conclude that these differ in any fundamental way from the ones we assume as relevant and important today? Are there surprises about what humans are enjoined to do in past times that stop us in our tracks? Are there rules of human behavior? On the basis of a particular set of texts and artifacts do we know about social organization? Is it hierarchical? Answers to such questions help us to focus our explanatory task by indicating the context in which we decide to approach the study in question.

The discovery of a new text is always an exciting event for the historian: it might be a new Shakespearean sonnet. Immediately our minds go to work. We might employ a pattern-matching algorithm to determine whether the use of words conforms to the use of words in the Shakespearean canon. It might be an ancient Sumerian text that prefigures images and narratives that occur in later documents. In fact, I can remember the shock of discovery when I studied the Enuma Elish for the first time and recognized its relationship to stories in the book of Genesis. It is no accident that cognitive anthropologists are interested in the process of cultural transmission and how stories are transmitted and transformed according to certain cognitive biases in the process of transmission.

One technique worth employing is that of determining the presence of relevant themes in newly discovered texts. Do they talk about an afterlife? Do they talk about mate choice, initiation, threats, or danger? If they talk about any, some, or all of these things, then we already possess a large amount of information about the cognitive capacities of the people who wrote and read these texts. We even know about such capacities in nonliterate societies that have artifacts and many forms of ritualized behavior, and much of the work that anthropologists have accomplished in such societies is of great value in throwing light not only on the forms but also on the capacities, which explain their origin and reception (Geertz 1994). We also know the importance of environmental and sociocultural triggers in eliciting certain types of thinking and certain forms of behavior. Of course, interpreting and explaining events

HISTORY IN SCIENCE

before the emergence of writing creates additional problems. Anthropologists who have studied nonliterate societies have solved part of the problem by participant and theoretically driven observation. But societies' long gone is another matter.

A case in point is the recent discovery of caves in South Africa, which contain an amazing number of partial skeletons of an early human species, *Homo naledi*, that seems to have performed ritual behavior. The important thing to note is that paleontologists already come with a great deal of knowledge to this situation. They already have a provisional classification and dating of all previous finds and clues about the kinds of behavior their specimens engaged in such as what foods they ate (by examining the wear and tear on teeth, for example), where they slept, whether or not they buried their dead, and so forth. A great deal of the work is comparative, comparing shapes of skulls, hands and feet, and overall posture. In the case of *Homo naledi*, it seems that bodies were placed in a very difficult-to-reach cave which requires an explanation and an interpretation. This has led to the hypothesis that this species practiced ritual burial because to bury someone in a difficult-to-reach cave is a deliberate, intentional act. It needs planning. Such arguments have already been going on for some time over whether Neanderthals buried their dead ritually. They certainly dug graves in which to place the deceased. What is important is that a scientist of human thought and behavior can appeal to evidence in terms of a hypothesis to confirm or disconfirm. If *Naledi* and Neanderthals both buried their dead, then it is possible to entertain the idea that ritual behavior at least is an early and widespread form of behavior among closely related species and not confined to *Homo sapiens*. Whether a ritual burial is a *religious* ritual burial is another matter.

All scientific knowledge is provisional. Some of it is quite firmly established. Other knowledge depends upon the complexity of the methods employed. Dating of paleontological objects is particularly difficult, but practitioners of these disciplines understand the problems and work to improve them.

The cognitive science of religion has been in the process of development since the 1970s. During this time, it has grown to be a recognized field of inquiry not only in the humanities and social sciences but even in the natural sciences. It has generated great arguments about the role that evolution plays in explaining religious thought and behavior and has precipitated a fruitful discussion about whether "religion" is a by-product or whether at least some of its features are adaptations. It has also triggered an argument about whether religion is a unified system of ideas or an aggregate concept where what is observable is but the surface feature of deep-seated cognitive dispositions, which results from the evolutionary history of our brain's development. There will be many more arguments in the future because as I have argued elsewhere, we have a progressive and not a degenerating research program. The most recent kid on the block is cognitive historiography which has a bright future and few of the impediments that often accompany the development of a new mode of inquiry. We should sing its praises.

I will now close this chapter, which stands as a tribute to my friend and colleague Armin Geertz, who came very early to recognize the power of addressing interesting subjects from a cognitive perspective and was willing to provide support and encouragement when few were listening as well as developing and establishing a solid program at Aarhus University.

References

Geertz, Armin W. (1994). *The Invention of Prophecy: Continuity and Meaning in Hope Indian Religion*, Los Angeles: University of California Press.

McCauley, Robert N., and E. Thomas Lawson (2007). "Cognition, Religious Ritual and Archaeology," in *The Archaeology of Ritual*, edited by Evangelos Kyriakidis, 209–54, Los Angeles: University of California Press, Cotsin Institute of Archaeology.

Mithen, Steven (1996). *The Prehistory of the Mind: The Cognitive Origins of Art, Religion and Science*, London: Thames and Hudson.

INTRODUCTION TO CHAPTER 11

I have placed the following chapter near the end of the book to contrast it to the first chapter, "Towards a Cognitive Science of Religion," at the book's beginning. The first chapter was brimming with excitement about this new scientific approach to religious thought and behavior, while this chapter is looking back after twenty years and explores whether the child has not only grown up but matured. I employ concepts in the philosophy of science to engage in the evaluation.

11

The Cognitive Science of Religion and the Growth of Knowledge

The mark of good science is its capacity to make our knowledge of the world grow. Philosophers of science have paid a great deal of attention to the issue of how our scientific knowledge of the world increases. For example, Imre Lakatos (1978), building on Karl Popper's *The Logic of Discovery* (1934), argued that there were two kinds of research programs that were either progressive or degenerative. Progressive research programs strengthen and increase explanatory power, leading to new forms of inquiry while maintaining a core set of principles, whereas degenerating programs decrease in explanatory power and ultimately produce less and less knowledge. Progressive research programs, therefore, are inferentially rich, represent growth in our knowledge of the world, and are a standard of excellence worthy of striving for. If that is the case, then it is worthwhile to examine new research programs in order to see whether they qualify as progressive. The cognitive science of religion provides a fine opportunity for such an examination. In its present state, it certainly seems to have made significant strides in the direction of inferentially rich knowledge. It is worth asking whether this putative accomplishment is apparent or real.

While this particular progressive research program started in the humanities, the scholars who began to think cognitively had for some time been paying attention to social-scientific explanations of religious thought and behavior but were dissatisfied with both the methods and the results of the various studies on the table. Much of social science had adopted an interpretive stance, which claimed that religious thought and behavior should be understood, not explained, while those who had explanatory interests insisted, under the influence of Durkheim, that only social facts could explain social facts. Fortunately, a revolution was occurring within the social sciences—the cognitive revolution—and it was this new way of explaining human thought and behavior in general that attracted a new generation of scholars. These cognitive thinkers, knowledgeable about the linguistic revolution that had shaken up the humanities, began to pay attention to new modes of psychological investigation in terms of the notion of information processing. What made the linguistic revolution interesting was its focus on the fact that languages were eminently sociocultural phenomena. If it could be shown that such collections of variation were, nevertheless, governed by a set of universal principles, then there was finally an exciting new way of looking at other cultural phenomena such as religions, which were also extensively varied, both historically and culturally.

So the cognitive science of religion, initially inspired by the achievements of the linguistic revolution, as well as by the reduction of behavioral psychology to cognitive psychology, rather quickly built theoretical relationships with the new social sciences such as cognitive psychology and eventually began a conversation with the newly developing cognitive anthropology and the emerging evolutionary psychology, as well as with the natural sciences, particularly the neurosciences and evolutionary biology. These connections led to questions and modes of inquiry at a number of levels of analysis, namely the social, psychological, and biological. The idea that only social facts could explain social facts was gleefully abandoned, as was the behaviorist notion that all explanatory variables were external to the organism. Autonomy and blank slates were, hopefully, put to rest.

Because of the conversation with cognitive scientists, whether they were philosophers, psychologists, anthropologists, or biologists, the initial focus of a new cognitive science of religion research program lay in finding ways to connect cognition and culture by approaching a subject matter "religion" that desperately needed an explanatory perspective rather than the purely interpretive approach that had characterized studies of religion at that point. Hence, what started out as a conversation between a few scholars in the humanities grasping rather tentatively the reins of science ended up with a veritable crowd of chariots charging around the scientific arena. It is not always clear that these risk-takers are now all participating in the same arena, but the excitement of the game is palpable.

How, then, has our knowledge of religion grown? First, simply by seeking better explanations than those provided by the autonomous social sciences, we were forced to connect sociocultural and psychological facts when looking at certain puzzling forms of thought and behavior. We were no longer satisfied to explain ritual behavior, for example, by appealing to socialization. It did not make sense to us that very widespread, cross-cultural phenomena just happened to be transmitted from generation to generation willy-nilly without paying attention to something that made people susceptible to certain ideas and the behavior associated with them. Second, as we began to develop new and more complex theories, it became apparent that the assumptions about "religion" as a coherent and systematic phenomenon was called into question because what we were learning from the cognitive, and eventually the evolutionary, sciences was that the mind that produced, entertained, and acquired religious concepts consisted of many different kinds of processing mechanisms that were sensitive and responsive to domain-specific information but not necessarily in any unified way.

This led us to pay attention to such cognitive mechanisms as animacy detection, agent detection, eye-gaze detection, face recognition, threat detection, contagion sensitivity, and many other psychological processes. For example, agency detection was a different cognitive process than either contagion sensitivity or fear-producing mechanisms, all of which, once identified, became relevant for the explanation of various forms of human thought and behavior in general and religious thought and behavior in particular.

It eventually became apparent that by focusing on cognitive mechanisms at the psychological level, we had better also take processes such as evolution on the biological level into consideration, because there had to be a story about how those mechanisms got there in the first place and what their significance and function were for survival and reproduction. What interdisciplinary scholars now saw was that we had to develop a cognitive and evolutionary science of religion if we were to continue to make our knowledge grow—a significant feature of an inferentially rich research program. And so a conversation among scholars in the humanities, specifically philosophers, historians, anthropologists, psychologists, and biologists, began to take place. All of those involved in these early stages were interested in why people all over the world were so willing to entertain very odd thoughts and engage in sometimes very bizarre behavior, while in other respects their judgments seemed quite veridical. The subject matter of "religion" was clearly on the table, but seen now as something genuinely puzzling, not just for those "primitives" hiding in the jungle but also in the churchly houses of the new world.

Let us focus on the issue of whether the subject matter "religion" is a coherent system. Why, for example, do some people find it important and relevant to perform a set of acts that they think involves agents with some very counterintuitive qualities when they initiate someone into a special age group? And how does this concept of such special agents come about? It is no secret that there is a very serious and extremely interesting argument going on about whether certain religious ideas or concepts (that either directly or indirectly inform certain types of behavior) are either instances of adaptations or at least linked pleiotropically to types of behavior that are adaptive (Sosis 2009). As Richard Sosis notes, those who came late to the cognitive science of religion encountered a well-established and highly influential by-product view of religious thought and behavior. An adaptationist approach by D. S. Wilson (2002) in his Darwin's Cathedral as Sosis points out, attacked not only the by-product view of the cognitive scientists of religion but the social-scientific views of Stark, Bainbridge, and Fink (e.g., Stark and Bainbridge 1996; Stark and Fink 1992). Not only did Wilson argue that religion is an adaptive phenomenon but also he employed the notion of group selection to fortify his case. Many who had taken evolutionary theory seriously thought that group selection explanations had never been particularly convincing and had, in fact, long since been abandoned by evolutionary scientists (West et al. 2007). Wilson not only insisted on the importance of group evolution but also failed to take the fact of cognitive mechanisms into account at all. In a sense he made a direct jump from the biological to the cultural, bypassing the psychological mechanisms that promised a bridge for a safer crossing for those committed to an interdisciplinary perspective.

Evolutionary biologists such as West, Griffin, and Gardner (2007) question the usefulness of group selection approaches to cooperation (which Wilson thinks is the main function of religion) and show how kin selection explains more formally and efficiently the various examples that Wilson raises and does so without the confusions that group selection approaches typically create.

The same cannot be said for psychologists such as Jesse Bering, who has performed psychological experiments that focused primarily on afterlife beliefs (2006). Bering does not argue that "religion" is adaptive as a group selectionist phenomenon, but only that a special set of beliefs about the afterlife may very well be. His experiments provide important clues as to why this might be the case. Sosis, however, intends to go the whole way and is now working on religion as a complex adaptive system. He sees "religion" as a coherent phenomenon and focuses on the notion of cooperation, placing

RELIGION AND THE GROWTH OF KNOWLEDGE

an emphasis on the notion of prosociality, a theme developed initially by Durkheim. Whether this will persuade the scientists who have developed the by-product approach, which has not only identified many different kinds of mechanisms but also tied these to evolutionary processes on the kin selection model (Boyer 2001), remains to be seen. There is clearly more than one route to evolution without having to adopt either a group selectionist perspective as does Wilson or to see religion as a complex adaptive system as proposed by Sosis. These questions are, of course, both theoretical and empirical, and much work remains to be done.

The central issue is whether we need to focus on a bundle of features as the unit of analysis, as Sosis (2009) suggests, or whether it makes more sense from an evolutionary perspective to focus on the garden-variety mechanisms as adaptive (given a notion of basic capacities in need of development by environmental triggers that calibrate them). And it will be important to recognize the temporal differences involved when the different capacities achieve their mature status and efficient functioning via calibration. For example, the false-belief test has a temporal aspect that comes to place around the age of four (but see Spelke and others for an earlier date). My view is that it is better, from a methodological perspective, to regard these mechanisms as separate modules, each with its own history. But pluralism is a good thing and ensures that important questions are not ignored. One of the marks of a progressive research program is that alternative avenues of investigation open up and lead not only to new answers but also to new questions.

Of particular importance in the inclusive cognitive and evolutionary research program (i.e., putting aside the differences between the adaptationists and the spandrelists as well as the debate between kin and group selectionists) is the question of what kinds of ideas held a transmission advantage. As long as you were interested in evolution and thought that the capacities that natural selection was kind enough to endow us with were sufficient to account for the persistence of some representations at the expense of others, this question made a lot of sense. The groundbreaking work here was that of Dan Sperber (1985), who developed a sophisticated account of cultural transmission in terms of the notion of an epidemiology of representations. Sperber provided powerful arguments for a precise account of cultural transmission, going against the notion of memes originally suggested by Richard Dawkins (2006) and presently championed by Dan Dennett (2006). Some of the experimental work confirms that minimally counterintuitive ideas have a transmission advantage because of their attention-grabbing abilities and our capacity to pay attention to novelty. They are counterintuitive enough to focus our attention but not so counterintuitive that they simply become noise. Despite the applicability of these ideas for explaining how the counterintuitiveness of religious ideas could be successfully transmitted and prove capable of explaining why religious practices persist, no matter what the cultural context, there were certain nagging problems that simply kept demanding our attention. What about cost?

Actually, the initial question that captured my attention was the one so nicely put by Dan Sperber in 1975 when he asked why we find so frequently in human societies the kind of symbolic activity (of which religious symbolism was an instance) where the means put into play seem to be disproportionate to the explicit or implicit end, whether this be knowledge, communication, or production. Surely, where the costs of a cultural form seem clearly to outweigh its benefits, one is required to explain the persistence of such an expensive form of human thought and behavior. Sperber provided an important account by distinguishing between dictionary, encyclopedic, and symbolic representations and later developed a very sophisticated notion of relevance (Sperber and Wilson 1986). We make our judgments on the basis of their relevance.

The issue of the costliness of certain forms of behavior has been developed in very interesting ways by Sosis. Some rituals can involve great expenditures of resources, cause great pain, and even put participants in danger. Do the benefits outweigh the costs? Sosis thinks that they do if they are sufficient to diminish the threat of free riders. I presume that the conclusion is that the prosocial benefits overcome the costs in the energy consumption ledger. This of course raises a larger question: Are we trying to show that religion is really a good thing or a bad thing? Durkheim, a long time ago, was criticized for providing a justification for religion rather than an explanation of it. Adaptationists sometimes seem to be suggesting that religion is a good thing because of its prosocial benefits. Dawkins (2006), on the other hand, thinks that religion is a bad thing because its social costs are enormous.

Actually, by-product theoreticians have not participated in this debate, first of all because they see religion as an aggregate phenomenon and argue that the unit of analysis is individual objects of selection, and second because, by focusing on the various individual mechanisms, they are able to point to the adaptive effects of these mechanisms without arguing that the by-products are adaptations. For example, it can be argued that agency detection is an important cognitive skill with great evolutionary advantages, without having to show that agents with some counterintuitive qualities are advantageous for survival and reproduction. (See, however, Michael Blume [2009].)

Of course, there are still scholars heavily influenced by Freudian thought, who continue to raise the issue of motivation. Are explanatory accounts that focus on cognitive mechanisms sufficient to explain motivation? I think that the answer is actually quite simple. The processes of evolution designed us to be susceptible to certain representations such as ritualized forms. We want to mark transitions from one state of affairs to another because they provide satisfaction. We want to think that there are hidden forces at work that are not available to the senses but might have dangerous consequences. While scientific theorizing and the sophisticated experimental work that accompanies it is dependent on our reflective capacities, our desire for knowledge is also driven by our intuitive capacities.

This leads me to an important issue that has played a significant role in the development of the cognitive and evolutionary science of religion—the distinction between intuitive and reflective knowledge. Evolution has designed us with a set of capacities capable of extensive calibration by input external to the organism, a set of expectations that lead, for example, to the acquisition of language, as well as various forms of folk knowledge (folk physics, folk biology, and folk psychology), that for the most part equip us to deal with the world around us. We can call this the capacity for generativity.

The issue of generativity raises the question of what capacity or capacities it took to produce the ideas that acted as candidates subject to the forces of selection. Was blind variation sufficient to account for the production of these ideas? Even if it was, we still need an account of the mechanisms that produced the variations. Perhaps we can agree that evolutionary theory has gone some way toward explaining how our cognitive capacities have acquired the form that they have. In the simplest terms, they consist of a set of biases or capacities strongly dependent on development and calibration by environmental variables that are valuable aids in increasing the probability of survival and reproductive success. While the cognitive capacity for the acquisition of language, originally developed by Noam Chomsky, is already on a firm footing, there are many other capacities that deserve our attention and have been the subject of investigation in the cognitive and evolutionary science of religion. Take, for instance, agency detection (alluded to earlier). The capacity to distinguish agents from everything else in the world is a notable evolutionary achievement that denotes significant advantages. In fact, this powerful mechanism detects not only agents but also kinds of agents. The infant in the cradle, sometimes referred to as the scientist in the crib (Gopnik, Meltzoff, and Kuhl 2000), is a remarkable creature, and clever experimental studies show how early in human development the capacities in question make their presence known.

Now we spandrelists have made much of the so-called hyperactivity of our agency detection system: HADD, as it has come to be known (initially suggested by McCauley at a conference on the island of Seili in Finland and developed by Stewart Guthrie [1993] and Justin Barrett [2004] in very fruitful ways). The basic idea is that if we have an agent detector mechanism running full tilt, then there are good reasons for it to become overactive in certain situations. Actually, I doubt whether we need to think of such a system as being hyperactive at all. Any detection mechanism worth its salt simply needs to be active enough to be sufficient for the job, that is, sufficient to have the capacity to distinguish agents from everything else in the world and attempt to compute their intentions. It simply needs to deliver slightly more false positives than negatives over the long haul to deliver a selective advantage. Consequently, some stimuli can trigger responses that suggest the presence of agents without any agents being there. The reason that they are taken seriously is because of the mechanism of decoupling, that is, we have no problem regarding real people we know are alive but not physically present. Their ontological status is not dependent on their immediate presence to the perceiver in question.

In any case, the contingent association between agency detection and danger, or if you will, threat to survival and reproduction, is of particular importance. Having the capacity to discriminate between friendly and unfriendly agents on the basis of available cues would clearly provide an organism with significant advantages. Joseph LeDoux (1998) has provided the classic study on the fearful response to imminent danger. Of much more interest, however, would be the capacity to be particularly responsive to potential danger. Running away, when you are being charged by a lion, while useful and potentially life enhancing, is far more energy intensive and costly than being clever enough to recognize the potential presence of a predator by learning to read its tracks and rapidly leaving the scene of the potential encounter with the predator. Learning to pay attention to eye gaze, or ear motion, or the various shapes that faces take for that matter might be even more fitness enhancing than responding to rapid movement toward you. For example, as I can testify from personal experience, elephants rhythmically flap their ears when they contemplate charging you. So, if they wiggle their ears vigorously, it is time to read the signs of potential danger and get out of the way before they charge. Waiting for the charge to occur before you remove yourself from the scene can be fatal. Or to take another example, being particularly sensitive to certain disgusting smells is certainly a useful aid to avoiding dangerous substances (Rozin, Haidt, and McCauley 1993).

Now I think that if we were endowed with the capacity to be even moderately responsive to potential danger, this would have implications for our understanding of certain forms of behavior that might be considered religious in nature. Initial work in this area has been done by Szechtman and Woody (2004) and Boyer and Lienard (2006). Both pairs of scientists were interested in ritualized behavior on a continuum from the behavior of ordinary people in special situations such as pregnancy where intrusive thoughts, for example, emerge naturally, to such examples as patients with obsessive-compulsive disorder. Work on ritualization has been very productive and has provided important clues about cultural rituals in general and religious rituals in particular. Developing this idea would not eliminate the spandrelistic character of the behavior, but it might show that culturally developed forms of such behavior would reflect or incorporate these tendencies, both thematically in the words spoken and behaviorally in the deeds done. What I have in mind here is not the compulsive focus on certain features in the environment requiring our attention, but the repetitive elements that seem to play such an important role in religious rituals. Mary Douglas, in Purity and Danger (1966), called our attention to the widespread phenomenon of symbolically polluting substances. What we need to do, however, is to broaden the concept of danger to include substances, individuals, and actions. Ethnographic work shows that in religious contexts all three are potentially dangerous and need to be ritually addressed. So I am arguing that there seems to be a close connection between such "symbolic" behavior and the kind of behavior in response to potential danger that we seem to be capable of recognizing and responding to. Sometimes we run from an actual predator; sometimes we run from a potential predator. And sometimes the latter action takes the shape of a dance around a fire as we sing a-wim-o-weh.

Then, of course, there is the issue of religious experience. There is no doubt that some people have special experiences that they deem religious. Certain scholars have suggested that an explanation of the origin and persistence of religion can be developed purely on the basis of experiences such as mysticism. Some neuroscientists have attempted to develop this idea by searching for structures in the brain that are dedicated to the production of such extraordinary experiences. These ideas emerge from the work of William James (1902) in his *The Varieties of Religious Experience* that certainly established the tradition for this form of inquiry. While I am willing to acknowledge that individuals who are susceptible to such experiences may make some contribution toward our accounts for the continued success of religious systems no matter what the cultural context is and no matter what level of hostility may be present, as a kind of role model, I think the fact remains that, from a sociological and psychological point of view, the vast number of religious participants have never had such experiences but find participation in religious ritual worthwhile anyway. Religious practices can do their job even if they have no meaning to the participants. As any anthropologist can tell you, a predictable answer to the question, "why do you do this in the way that you do?" is "because it is the custom." Of course, some religious traditions make meaning of something that is of great importance. An elaborate hermeneutic tradition can develop with elaborate theologies. However, theologies, an example of reflective thought, are not necessary for religious ideas to work.

A notion of theological correctness has been developed in significant ways by Justin Barrett and Frank Keil (1996) and developed by Jason Slone (2007). The notion here is that even though people, when they reflect on their own ideas and behavior, develop certain norms, have a set of concepts that they regard as a kind of orthodoxy, or are right thinking about counterintuitive agents, for example, reveal, under experimental conditions, that their quick and dirty judgments are governed by their intuitions and not their reflections. In fact, the notion of cognitive biases is intimately connected with our notions about intuitive and reflective capacities generally and it plays a role not only in the cognitive science of religion but also in such disciplines as behavioral economics.

While the original insights of the cognitive science of religion were largely theoretical with some attention paid to empirical issues, primarily historical and ethnographic reports, it was clear that experimental studies would have to be done in order to support this new way of looking at religious thought and behavior. One of the earliest was by Barrett and Lawson (2001), which was designed to confirm or disconfirm hypotheses about peoples' intuitive knowledge about ritual behavior. This experiment made three predictions: (1) people with little or no knowledge of any given ritual system would have intuitions about the potential effectiveness of a ritual given minimal information about the structure of ritual, (2) the representation of superhuman agency in the action structure would be considered the most important factor contributing to effectiveness, and (3) an appropriate intentional agent initiating the action would be considered relatively more important than any specific action performed. The results of the study supported the Lawson and McCauley predictions (1990) and suggested that our expectations regarding ordinary social actions apply to religious rituals. This provided grist for the by-product approach to the study of religion. Since that early study, there have been a host of experimental studies testing various predictions that have emerged from the development of the cognitive science of religion.

In conclusion, we may now ask the question again: Is the cognitive and evolutionary science of religion a progressive research program that has made a contribution to the growth of our scientific knowledge or a biological, psychological, and cultural phenomenon such as religious thought and behavior or not? From the evidence presented here, I think that the answer is a definite yes. The research program has found new and interesting ways to connect cognition and culture. Moreover, it has also connected cognition with evolutionary explanations. It has developed both notions of religious thought and behavior as a by-product and also entertained the idea of certain cognitive features as being adaptive. The caveat here is that some avenues are not as progressive as others. The by-product approach, particularly when focusing on various different capacities, has painted a far broader and more interesting picture of religion than one simply focused on prosociality. The cognitive and evolutionary science of religion has laid the ground for a serious examination of the notions of religion either as an aggregate phenomenon or as a complex

RELIGION AND THE GROWTH OF KNOWLEDGE

adaptive system. My view is that the former is the more useful and productive approach.

The cognitive science of religion has also shown that good ethnography recognizes the differences between peoples' intuitive and reflective beliefs and a good psychology focuses on our evolutionarily endowed capacities that are subject to calibration by various environmental and cultural variables. And it has explained how much of our knowledge of the world is determined through the intricate processes of cultural transmission. We now have in place the scientific tools for further growth in our knowledge.

References

Barrett, J. (2004). *Why Would Anyone Believe in God?* Walnut Creek: AltaMira Press.

Barrett, J., and F. Keil (1996). "Conceptualising a Non-Natural Entity: Anthrtopomorphism in God Concepts," *Cognitive Psychology* 31 (30): 219–47.

Barrett, J., and E. T. Lawson (2001). "Ritual Intuitions: Cognitive Contributions to Judgments of Ritual Efficacy," *Journal of Cognition and Culture* 1 (2): 183–201.

Blume, M. (2009). "The Reproductive Effects of Religious Affiliation," in *The Biological Evolution of Religious Mind and Behavior*, edited by E. Voland and W. Schifenhovel, 117–21, New York: Springer Frontiers Collection.

Boyer, P. (2001). *Religion Explained: Evolutionary Origins of Religious Thought*, New York: Basic Books.

Boyer, P., and Lienar, P. (2006). "Why Ritualized Behavior? Precaution Systems and Action Parsing in Developmental, Pathological and Cultural Rituals." *Behavioral and Brain Sciences* 19 (6): 595–613.

Dawkins, R. (2006). *The God Delusion*, London: Bantam Press.

Dennett, D. (2006). *Breaking the Spell: Religion as a Natural Phenomenon*, New York: Viking.

Douglas, M. (1966). *Purity and Danger: An Analysis of Concepts of Pollution and Taboo*, New York: Praeger.

Gopnik, A., A. Meltzoff, and P. Kuhl (2000). *The Scientist in the Crib*, New York: Harper Collins.

Guthrie, S. (1993). *Faces In the Clouds: A New Theory of Religion*, New York: Oxford University Press.

James, w. (1902). *The Varieties of Religious Experience*, New York: Modern Library.

Lakatos, I. (I978). *The Methodology of Scientific Research Programmes.* Volume 1 *Philosophical Papers*, edited by J. Worrall and G. Currie, Cambridge: Cambridge University Press.

Lawson, E. T., and R. N. McCauley (1990). *Rethinking Religion: Connecting Cognition and Culture*, Cambridge: Cambridge University Press.

Le Doux, J. E. (1998). *The Emotional Brain: The Mysterious Underpinnings of Emotional Life*, New York: Simon and Shuster.

Popper, K. (1934). *The Logic of Scientific Discovery*, New York: Harper and Row.

Rozin, P., j. Haidt, and C. R. McCauley (1993). "Disgust," in *Handbook of Emotions*, edited by M. Lewis and J. M. Haviland, 69–73, New York: Guilford.

Slone, D. J. (2007). *Theological Incorrectness: Why Religious People Believe what they Shouldn't*, Oxford: Oxford University Press.

Sosis, R. (2009). "The Adaptationist-By-Product Debate on the Evolution of Religion. Fiuve misunderstandings of the Adaptationist Program," *Journal of Cognition and Culture* 9 (3): 315–32.

Sperber, D. (1985). *On Anthropological Knowledge*, Cambridge: Cambridge University Press.

Sperber, D., and D. Wilson (1986). *Relevance: Communication and Cognition*, Cambridge, MA: Harvard University Press.

Stark, R., and R. Finke (1992). *Acts of Faithj: Explaining the human side of Religion*, Oakland: Univerisity of California Press.

Stark, R. W., and D. S. Bainbridge (1996). *A Theory of Religion*, New Brunswiuck: Rutgers University Press.

Szechtman, H., and E. Woody (2004). "Obsessive and Compulsive Disorder as a Disturbance of Security Motivation," *Psychological Review* III (1): 111–27.

West, S. A., A. S. Griffin, and A. Gardner (2007). "Social Semantics: How Helpful has Group Selection Been?" *Journal of Evolutionary Biology* 21 (3): 374–85.

Wilson, D. S. (2002). *Darwin's Cathedral: Evolution, Religion and the Nature of Society*, Chicago: Chicago University Press.

INTRODUCTION TO CHAPTER 12

This is that chapter that I referred to in Chapter 3. It is an appeal for historians to take cognitive science in general and cognitive psychology in particular very seriously. To do so will require engaging in a conversation with scholars in various disciplines. Of course, whenever the appeal goes out to break out of the confines of a particular discipline and engage in cross- and interdisciplinary work, a search for concepts and methods that work in more than one place and in more than one way is absolutely necessary. The historians that I know such as Luther Martin have done the work. They understand that history is the flow of time. That the transmission of ideas takes minds not only to formulate ideas but to transmit them and receive them and also to decode them. And that knowing how minds work enriches historical accounts. I doubt whether an account of religiosity is possible without an account of the changes in the types of religiosity over the centuries as well as an account of the underlying persistence of certain key concepts such as agents with special qualities.

12

Counterintuitive Notions and the Problem of Transmission

The Relevance of Cognitive Science for the Study of History

Religious narratives are cluttered with collections of counterintuitive claims. Animals speak, people rise from the dead, old women leave their bodies at home at night and almost instantaneously appear elsewhere to wreak sickness and death on those who have offended them, invisible beings fly through the air on banana leaves, diviners read the future, and prophets declare the end of the world. Such claims seem to violate our views of what the world is like, a world in which animals don't speak, dead people stay dead, and only news commentators predict future trends.

Having studied such notions in their cultural context, many anthropologists have noted that such claims are taken to be counterintuitive not merely by the anthropologist in the field but even by the people who hold them. Philosophers and comparative religionists have also revealed their puzzlement about the nature of such claims, and many have committed their intellectual lives to projects designed to plumb their semantic depths.

The presence of such notions not only in societies where oral traditions predominate but also in literate societies continues to precipitate vigorous debates in the social sciences and humanities. How are we to interpret them? How to explain their origin, describe their structure, and account for their persistence? Philosophers and anthropologists have engaged each other in extensive discussion about such matters; I refer particularly to the so-called rationality debate.[11] In fact, a veritable cloud of theories much larger than a man's hand has gathered on the academic horizon raining symbolist, intellectualist, emotivist, functionalist, ideologist, phenomenologist, structuralist, and postmodernist approaches, each promising to quench the thirst of the perplexed student of religion. Few expect the clouds to evaporate soon. And that is the way it should be. Inquirers appreciate the inclement weather provided by problematic knowledge. The light from the sun of complete knowledge would be dangerous to the mind's eye.

What is not so obvious is that historians also have a stake in this debate. At stake is the problem of the transmission of ideas and the practices they inform. While it is easy enough to explain the transmission of common sense ideas, the persistence of radically counterintuitive notions in even the most putatively enlightened of cultures poses a problem of the first order for scholars in the humanities and social sciences. Of course, simple-minded answers are always ready to hand: human beings are basically irrational, our animal nature is always waiting to pop out like the proverbial jack-in-a-box, all knowledge is relative anyway, and so on.

Even more complex answers, such as those provided by psychoanalysis and Marxist theory, are easily available, but their lack of scientific rigor (i.e., a failure to demonstrate their systematicity, coherence, and testability), while a plus for many humanists, has failed to persuade theorists of a more scientific bent of their viability. But even if these harsh judgments turn out to be premature, who can doubt that these traditions of thought do little more than restate the problem rather than providing fruitful solutions to it. At most, such approaches simply try to make it disappear by relocation.

Other appeals also wait in the wings, most especially the appeal to context. The hope seems to lie in the pious belief that if we could specify the context for the appearance of such counterintuitive claims, then we could account for their origin, structure, and persistence. The trouble is that while knowledge of the context may very well provide the necessary conditions for theorizing about counterintuitive ideas, it is incapable of identifying the sufficient conditions for their appearance and persistence in human history. This is particularly troublesome when we realize the severe criticism constantly bombarding counterintuitive ideas by the intellectual elite in many cultures, especially our own.

One of the main reasons for treating the appeal to context pessimistically is quite simply that contexts are not causal structures. Rather, they are webs or networks, indefinitely large in compass, which do nothing more than provide the background against which particular historical phenomena emerge. As such they are incapable of acting as mechanisms capable of producing effects.[2]

Even if in our appeal to contexts, we propose constraints on them, for example, by confining our inquiries to political, economic, or even the intellectual systems, we still have not identified structures capable of accounting for their emergence, development, and persistence. One reason is that in the same constrained context, *different* religious ideas and the practices they inform emerge. Of course, we can keep piling on constraints, but the moment will come when we will have lost the notion of context completely and will find ourselves staring into the face of a particular idea or a particular act with vast ramifications. The obviously metaphorical work that the notion of "context" has supposedly been accomplishing will suddenly be recognized for what it is, a world of connotation with no denoting value.

So to repeat the problem: if we grant any validity to the notion of civilization at all, how do we then account for the persistence of counterintuitive notions in the very context of enlightenment with its reputation for casting out the darkness?

Why Do Bizarre Notions Persist?

Historians have often been only too willing to assign the problem of the persistence of counterintuitive notions to psychologists, anthropologists, philosophers, theologians, or, in desperation, the therapeutically inclined. But they do so at the expense of recognizing that *if they are willing to make assumptions about the transmission of tradition, then it is their job to help in identifying the mechanisms which underwrite such a process.* One thing is certain, historians can no longer assume that the simple-minded psychology of past generations will provide the mechanism of transmission. The time for passive minds, or blank Lockean slates, acting as conduits of sociocultural information has long disappeared. Neither recent behaviorist nor cognitivist psychologies (in either ecological or information-theoretic forms) will license such simplistic assumptions. Current psychological theorizing about perceptual and conceptual processes discloses the extreme complexity of our cognitive mechanisms and the role they play in structuring our experience. The findings of experimental psychology certainly will not permit the kind of transmission that historians would like to have.

Pascal Boyer has made a significant contribution to this discussion by adopting a cognitive stance in theorizing about counterintuitive phenomena. He argues that *counterintuitive notions become more readily explicable when viewed against the background of a set of deeply ingrained intuitive assumptions acquired very early in conceptual development.* His argument is that before we can account for the persistence of the counterintuitive ideas which continually surface in every society we need to understand the nature of intuitive ideas. Specifically, Boyer resists the temptation to dissociate counterintuitive ideas from their relationship to our common sense notions about the kinds of things and processes there are in the world. In fact, Boyer shows that when we analyze our intuitive assumptions about the kinds of things there are in the world, we make the remarkable discovery that their cognitive appearance is underdetermined by cultural instruction. Anthropologists in the field, when asking the right question, discover that *people almost always know more than they have been taught.*[3] Boyer argues that it makes sense to see such principles as structuring experience rather than being derived from it.

Boyer has also made a case for the domain specificity of such intuitive assumptions. This means that (1) the principles which determine such assumptions are activated at different stages of conceptual development and (2) the processes of inference about different domains are relatively independent of each other. So, for example, inferences about the kinds of things that exist (ontological inferences) are relatively independent of inferences about causal processes. If we take the word of developmental psychologists, it seems, for example, that our assumptions about the kinds of things that exist (persons, animals, plants, artifacts, and so forth) are acquired at different stages and in different ways from our notions of what makes what happen.

Boyer appeals to the findings of experimental psychology, particularly theories of psychological development, to support such claims. Boyer's view about domain specificity is designed to undercut both cultural relativism and constructivist theories of the acquisition of knowledge which argue for a kind of lock-step cognitive development cutting across various domains. As Boyer concludes:

> Intuitive principles are domain-specific and trigger functionally different cognitive processes, depending on the domain. In other words, conceptual development does not imply applying an all-purpose, "theory-making" cognitive device to a variety of available stimuli. On the contrary, it implies applying significantly different cognitive heuristics to different domains.[4]

About fourteen years ago, quite independently of Boyer, Robert McCauley and I (inspired by Chomsky's investigations into the structure of natural languages, disturbed by the contextualism gaining ascendancy in both history and anthropology, intrigued by the work of Dan Sperber on symbolism, and taking note, furthermore, both of the movement in philosophy to naturalize epistemology and of the revolution in cognitive psychology) began to work on a project that was later published as *Rethinking Religion: Connecting Cognition and Culture*.[5] This work was intended to give a cognitive account of religious ritual systems. Although we freely acknowledged the contributions earlier theories had made to our understanding of religion, particularly ritual, we thought the time had come to utilize the new strategies and theories made available by the revolution precipitated by the productive development of the cognitive sciences.

We were particularly intrigued by the ease with which people seemed to acquire religious ideas at quite a young age regardless of cultural context and historical period, their ability to live ritual lives effortlessly despite intense political and economic pressures to the contrary, and their capacity to make judgments about ritual form with little explicit instruction. During the process of writing *Rethinking Religion*, we came to the conclusion that the *implicit* knowledge that people had of their own ritual systems and demonstrated by their capacity to make informed judgments about such systems could be described and analyzed by some of the techniques and strategies standardly employed in cognitive studies. We further concluded that this could be done with intriguing results for scholars in both the humanities and the social sciences, and most particularly for historians of religions.

We also thought that such an approach could lead not merely to a more sophisticated description of religious ritual systems but to their explanation. Of course, we were in complete agreement with the kind of sentiments recently expressed by Frank Keil about explanatory theorizing when he wrote: "No theory can ever hope to continuously make principled distinctions among all the possible entities it applies to; at some point the theory 'runs dry.'"[6] But we were also convinced that theorizing about the origin, structure, and persistence of religion had not yet reached such a cul-de-sac. If anything, the theoretical stream still was little more than a trickle compared to the flood of theories in the advanced sciences.

In our book, we adopted the controversial thesis that religious participants' *knowledge of ritual form could, for the most part, be analyzed independently of its meaning.* We did *not* think that the problem of the meaning of rituals should either be eliminated or ignored (in fact we devoted an entire chapter to semantic issues), but we did think that either starting with or focusing exclusively upon the problem of their meaning before having analyzed their form seemed to lead to semantic excess and problematic appeals to context. Simply put, we were more concerned with the underlying forms that religious phenomena take regardless of their meaning and despite their context.

One obvious reason for focusing upon form rather than meaning is that even when meaning is vague, problematic, or absent, people nevertheless continue to practice their rituals and expect others to do the same. Another reason for paying attention to participants' implicit knowledge of ritual form is that it provided the opportunity to identify principles of sufficient generality having cross-cultural significance. In other words, we were searching for general principles of sufficient scientific interest to aid our understanding of persistent features of human thought and practice.

In addition, we argued that peoples' *mental representations of religious ritual action differed in few significant ways from their representation of action generally.* A further reason for adopting this posture was our wish to counter the tendency of some scholars to make the object of religion, the subject of religion, or the method for the explanation of religion unique, autonomous, and radically distinct from other forms of human inquiry. Hence, we tried to show that *the representation of ritual action and the representation of action generally could largely be accomplished by the same means, namely by accessing basic categories such as agents, actions, and objects and the qualities and properties of such.* Furthermore, we argued that our representation of action constrained the acquisition of notions about religious action. In sum, rather than requiring special properties of either mind or culture to represent religious ritual forms, we were willing to propose that our basic, garden-variety cognitive equipment sufficed. And what better place to look for a sophisticated characterization of the nature of cognition than to the cognitive sciences?

One consequence of our analysis was to lessen the estrangement between religious and everyday thought. In other words, the significance of these claims lay in their potential for deflating the desperate attempts of scholars in the human sciences, especially those in comparative religion, to root religious notions in some a priori set of genetically generated religious notions, to differentiate radically religious knowledge from other forms of knowledge, to plead for some special epistemological and ontological realm forever safe from the prying eyes of the scientifically inclined, or to think that the mere appeal to context would provide the conditions sufficient for the explanation of the emergence of counterintuitive ideas and the practices they inform.

Who by now could fail to note the unbridled enthusiasm with which some historians of religion had welcomed the collapse of scientific pretensions by anthropologists who had decided to invade the hermeneutic hall of mirrors in response to their crisis of conscience.[7] Such joy at the funeral of certain forms of social science certainly gave pause to us who still thought that scientific theorizing about religion in general and ritual in particular was not only possible but desirable.

It was with considerable enthusiasm, therefore, that we found that Boyer had reached similar conclusions by an independent route. Both projects seemed to suggest that no matter what kind of position we adopted about a nativist account of intuitive assumptions, at least counterintuitive religious notions did not seem to require a nativist account for their explanation. In other words, even if a convincing case could be made that intuitive ontologies were the structures of experience rather than being derived from it, the counterintuitive features of religious ontologies did not themselves require their innateness. In fact, it would be remarkable if they did. At the same time, we did not think that a mere appeal to autonomous social facts excised from their psychological undergirding could resolve the problem of the origin, structure, and persistence of religious ritual forms.

Boyer's recent work, at least that represented in *The Naturalness of Religious Ideas*, extends his analysis put forward in *Tradition as Truth and Communication* by building on current developmental studies in psychology, especially those of Keil.[8] These studies seem to show not only an early but also a differential development of the conceptual structure.

Boyer argues that three cognitive domains are particularly relevant for developing an explanatory understanding of the counterintuitive claims of religions. According to Boyer, these domains involve the representation (1) of certain properties of physical objects and motion, (2) of the particular features of living things, and (3) of mental entities and processes. In a recent (unpublished) essay, he has developed an exhaustive "cognitive catalog of the supernatural" in which he shows how our ordinary categories of persons, animals, plants, physical, and artifactual objects *naturally* give rise to counterintuitive ideas, especially religious representations.

Boyer's point is that our ordinary ontological categories are violated only in some respects in religious situations. The fact that they violate *some* features of our ordinary categories makes them *attention demanding*, but the fact that they by and large maintain most of the features of our ordinary categories makes them *learnable*. Together, their attention-grabbing quality and their learnability ensure their memorability and, therefore, their transmissibility.

Our account of religious ritual form in *Rethinking Religion*, however, while compatible with Boyer's, emphasizes a set of representations implied by Boyer's list but to which he did not assign particular prominence, namely the notion of *agency*. In our work, McCauley and I argue that *the notion of agency is crucial for developing an explanatory understanding of religious ritual systems*. In fact, we claim that the acquisition of the notion of agency *constrains* the acquisition of religious notions.

In our view, religious rituals presuppose a fundamental role for a special class of agents, namely culturally postulated superhuman agents. As we have said elsewhere, this substantive commitment concerning religion is tantamount to offering a definition. This does not mean that we set great store in arguing endlessly over definitions, since we hold that definitions are grounded in explanatory theories and are not too interesting apart from their contribution to those theories' explanatory accomplishments. In fact, definitions are only as good as the theories that inspire them. Correspondingly, those theories are only as good as the problem-solving power, explanatory suggestiveness, generality, and empirical testability of their principles.[9]

Of course, some scholars in both comparative religion and anthropology will immediately claim that a religion such as Buddhism is a religion in which there are no beliefs in superhuman agents,[10] or, in their more cautious moments, that superhuman agents play little if any role in Buddhism. This is indeed a hoary and rather wrong-headed claim which perpetuates a highly elitist interpretation of Buddhism by concentrating primarily on a skewed reading of the texts and by reducing Buddhism to abstract theological speculation. If there were any doubt about the superhuman agency of even the Buddha himself, we would only have to note Robert Lester's words:

> Many extraordinary feats are attributed to the Buddha. He exorcized disease-causing spirits from a city, he preached while walking in the sky. He instantaneously quieted a mad elephant; he outwitted the great magicians of his time. In one of the most spectacular events of his ministry, the Buddha ascended into the heavens to preach the Dharma to his mother where she resided among the gods. After three months he descended to the earth triumphantly on a jeweled staircase accompanied by the Brahmanical gods Brahma and Indra.[11]

These ideas occur in a religious tradition that supposedly has no beliefs about superhuman agents!

Since writing *Rethinking Religion*, McCauley and I, like Boyer, have begun to evaluate the significance of a number of important findings in developmental psychology about conceptual structure in preverbal children, especially about the nature of memory. The findings of certain psychologists are relevant both for the problem of the nature and acquisition of conceptual structure and for the persistence of counterintuitive ideas through time. With regard to the first of these, we have taken particular note of the claim by developmental psychologists that children very early in life are capable of recognizing not only the distinction between nonliving and living things but also their recognition of agency.[12] These findings have strengthened our convictions about the fundamental role that superhuman agency plays in the representation of religious ritual action. Furthermore, these findings fit into a larger argument for making religious materials memorable and, therefore, culturally transmittable.

Ritual Form

And now let me lay out our plan for dealing with religious ritual form. First, at the most general methodological level, our strategy involves reversing Dilthey's insight that you cannot understand mind unless you understand culture by proposing that you cannot understand culture unless you understand mind.

If this tactic proves to be productive (and there is now enough evidence in the cognitive sciences to warrant claims about the productivity of cognitive methods), then those of us concerned with the explanation of cultural phenomena such as religious rituals need to pay particular attention to theories of mind which do justice to the mind's obvious complexity. Specifically, this means developing theories about cultural phenomena on the basis of the analysis of conceptual structure and process and then applying their results to the representation of ritual action. As McCauley and I have argued in "Connecting the Cognitive and the Cultural: Artificial Minds as Methodological Devices in the Study of the Socio-Cultural,"[13] Competence theorizing provides a particularly convenient form for analyzing such systems of representation because it permits us to employ *a normative judgment strategy* as a basic component of competence theorizing.

Human minds are the repositories of extensive knowledge about sociocultural structures. If all of such knowledge were explicit or conscious, then our main job as scholars would be to *organize* it from some theoretical perspective. Most such knowledge, however, is not conscious but implicit. It is not consciously entertained by the participants, and any attempt to elicit it from participants ends in failure. It is much like trying to ascertain the grammar of a newly discovered language by asking its speakers to identify the syntax of their language. Because this knowledge is implicit, it calls for special strategies to elicit it. The *normative judgment strategy* does this by neutralizing the idiosyncratic elements that inevitably emerge when we study individual minds in their sociocultural context. Positively, it enables the scholar to identify peoples' implicit knowledge revealed by their acquisition of and successful participation in their ritual systems as well as their judgments about real and possible uses of the underlying forms which structure such systems. Unlike some competence theorists, who seem willing to remain at the level of high abstraction, we think that performance considerations are crucial and cannot simply be swept under the methodological rug—hence our attention to the findings in developmental psychology which concentrate on cognitive performance.

Second, as I have already indicated, our theory analyzes a number of features of religious ritual form independently of any meanings that hermeneutically or theologically inclined scholars attempt to assign to such structures. For that matter, the theory attends to aspects of ritual form, which are independent of the content that ritual participants may attribute to them. In explaining religious ritual, meaning does not matter! For example, *it is not necessary to know what a ritual act means in order to know that it cannot be performed unless another act has been performed before it*. All that needs to be done in order to recognize this fact is a little fieldwork. Trips to exotic lands are not required; the local grocery store will do. People usually know what they have to do ritually, even if they have no view of the contents of ritual action.

There are several reasons for making such methodological moves: (1) while ritual form is *relatively* stable, ritual content is remarkably variable not only cross-culturally but intraculturally as well, and (2) we wish to counter the tendency of those—especially philosophers and theologians—who overemphasize semantic issues and the role of interpretation when unpacking them. As Dan Sperber has argued, the problem is not what symbols mean but how symbolism works. Explaining the latter involves more than hermeneutic circling. At a minimum, such theorizing involves modeling cognitive structures and processes and demonstrating their explanatory role in forms of human behavior. Furthermore, paying attention to cognitive models is as much a matter of psychological explanation as it is the intuitive divining of social meanings "from the participants' point of view."

Third, our theory is an exercise in cognitive modeling with three further goals: (1) to provide a dear and efficient way of describing the mental representations of religious participants about the form of their ritual actions largely independent of their content, (2) to devise a set of categories and principles which constrain ritual form, and (3) to make predictions about important features of ritual form as these are ideally represented in the minds of ritual participants and often mirrored in their performance. The outcome of this project consists in a single set of principles in a unified theory capable of accounting for important features of religious ritual systems.

Constraints on Ritual Action

Let us examine some of these goals:

1. In *the representation of religious ritual form,* we formulate a system which is capable of representing action in general and ritual action in particular by exploiting a set of rules and categories which generate abstract structural descriptions for such representations.[14] Bluntly, our principles produce nice tree diagrams that enable us either to identify important, but not always obvious, relationships among religious ritual acts, or to ask the kinds of questions *of participants* which will indicate their implicit knowledge of the underlying forms. Such knowledge can be elicited by asking them to make judgments about specific ritual situations. Our approach gives us the means to identify not only who the agents in a ritual are but also their qualities. It also permits us to distinguish among ritual agents, the actions they perform, and the logical objects of such acts. Further, our method allows us to specify the qualities and properties of the actions in which the ritual consists. In addition to such an *action representation system,* we postulate a *conceptual scheme* which provides *content* to the constituents of the system for the representation of action. Obviously, different conceptual schemes in different historical and cultural situations will supply different content, ensuring, thereby, the acknowledgment of cultural variability. Finally, we specify a set of universal principles which constrain the products of the cognitive system for the representation of action and consequently for the representation of religious ritual action.

2. As I have already indicated, *one principle and category, which specifies and constrains ritual action and makes predictions about them possible,* is *the principle of superhuman agency.* This involves the character of the superhuman agent's involvement in the ritual. One of the consequences of our theory is the prediction that those rituals where superhuman agents function actively in the ritual will be judged by participants to be more central to a religious system than where, for example, such agents assume a more passive role such as receiving a sacrifice. These are empirical matters which can be tested in the field.

Another principle which constrains ritual action is *the principle of superhuman immediacy.* In fact, this principle constrains the application of the first principle. It shows that the fewer the enabling actions to which appeal must be made by a member of a religious tradition in order to implicate a superhuman agent, the more fundamental the ritual is to the religious system. It should be obvious that such judgments by religious ritual participants will not always conform to theological expectations.

Our theory also permits us to make predictions about other features of ritual form, for example, their repeatability and reversibility. In addition, our theory predicts that the greater the number of culturally postulated superhuman agents in a religious system, the more ritually rich it will be in comparison to systems with fewer agents (e.g., monotheistic, bitheistic, and tritheistic systems).

In short, our methodological strategy takes a system of mental representations as its theoretical object, employs the strategies of the cognitive sciences to characterize those representations, and argues that participants' mental representations of their ritual acts are overwhelmingly grounded in the system they employ for the representation of action generally. For those interested in identifying the causes of religious ritual behavior, at least part of the cause of such behavior lies in the role that such ritual systems play.

This latter point about the representation of action connects with the recent findings in developmental psychology alluded to earlier, in particular, the work of Jean Mandler. Her studies of early infancy show that preverbal children not only recognize the difference between animacy and inanimacy, but, more significantly for our purposes, represent the concept of agency. In fact, according to Mandler, early conceptual achievements are quite impressive and include not only animacy and inanimacy but also causality, agency, containment, and support. It is not just that infants quite quickly demonstrate their ability to represent the world in terms of the kinds of things that there are in the world—for example, things that start themselves and things that require other things to get them going. Rather, they also very early develop the concept of agency. This involves the notion of an animate object which can change its own status, for example, its location, but can also cause another object, either animate or inanimate, to change its status (e.g., its location). The significant point here is that while all agents are animate, not all animate things are automatically thought of as agents. They become agents when they act in such a manner that they effect an alteration in state. Birds and butterflies are represented as animate because they fly through the air. It is only when they make small twigs bounce when they land or flowers tremble as they remove nectar that they are represented as agents. Agents not only get inanimate things to do things but animate ones as well. With such notions in place so early, it should not be surprising that people can acquire notions of special classes of agents, actions, and objects.

Boyer argues that "the most obvious and most probably the most common way in which religious ideas can be counter-intuitive . . . is the postulation of a class of beings whose specific properties make them, either very strange physical objects, or apparently non-physical ones." He goes on to assert correctly that religious systems are almost invariably based on such assumptions. So much so that the idea of nonphysical beings has often been taken from Tylor onwards, as the very definition of religion.[15] This is an important insight about the counterintuitive qualities of such beings, but it is not enough. It is my view that Boyer misses the more important point that such a class of culturally postulated beings is consistently viewed as composed of agents capable of acting upon logical objects and leading to specific culturally postulated consequences. It is not simply the notion of animate beings projected onto superhuman beings in rather odd ways that is at stake, but the representation of agents extended to include superhuman agents who by their special abilities are capable of bringing about consequences of which ordinary agents are incapable.

If the developmental findings referred to earlier hold up, then, in fact, they provide important clues as to why religious notions such as "the gods" are easily acquired, namely that beliefs in superhuman agents are easily acquired: the notion of agents is easily acquired, and once a notion is acquired, humans tend to extend them to new domains. Of course, ideas that are easily acquired and extended are more memorable and transmittable than ones that are not.

Other findings, not from developmental psychology but from cognitive linguistics, also seem to be relevant to our claim about the fundamental importance of agency. I have in mind Ronald Langacker's work.[16] I regard Langacker's account of a prototypical action, which he takes as central to the grammars underlying all natural languages and which involves a basic analysis of action, to be almost identical to our own. Langacker says:

> A claim of the framework is the symbolic nature of grammatical units. Like other symbolic elements, the grammatical notions that concern us are characterized with reference to cognitive domains. Among these domains are certain abstract but nonetheless powerful folk models pertaining to the make-up of our world, the transmission of energy and its role in driving events and the nature of canonical actions. These models are part of our conceptual apparatus; they are not solely (or even primarily) linguistic.[17]

Langacker's point is that the very structure of language itself presupposes such fundamental conceptual notions.

It should be apparent, therefore, that a cognitive approach, which pays attention to the role that human minds play in the production of cultural forms such as religious ritual, promises to add to our knowledge of such rituals. If such promises continue to be fulfilled, we are in the process of deepening our knowledge of religion and its persistence in human history.

Notes

1 Wilson (1970).

2 Of course, if we are willing to distinguish between the form of such ideas and their contents, then what contexts do is to supply the contents for such ideas. But it is the emergence of the form that requires explanation, namely, why do counterintuitive ideas keep cropping up no matter what the context.

3 See Sperber (1975), and Lawson (1993).

4 Boyer (1994).

5 Lawson and McCauley (1990).

6 Keil (1989).

7 Lawson and McCauley (1993).

8 Boyer (1990).

9 Lawson and McCauley (1993: 217).

10 Humphrey and Laidlaw (1994).

11 Lester (1987: 68).

12 See the work of Mandler, particularly (1992).

13 McCauley and Lawson (1993).

14 See Chapter 5 of *Rethinking Religion* for a complete discussion of these principles, pp. 84–136.

15 Boyer (unpublished).

16 Langacker (1990).

17 Langacker (1990: 215).

References

Boyer, Pascal (1990). *Tradition as Truth and Communication*, Cambridge: Cambridge University Press.

Boyer, Pascal (1994). *The Naturalness of Religious Ideas*, 110, Berkeley: Berkeley University Press.

Boyer, Pascal (unpublished). "Religion and the Bounds of Sense: A Cognitive Catalogue of the Supernatural."

Humphrey, Caroline and James Laidlaw (1994). *The Archetypal Actions of Ritual*, New York: Oxford University Press.

Keil, Frank C. (1989). *Concepts, Kinds, and Cognitive Development*, 277, Cambridge: Cambridge University Press.

Langacker, Ronald W. (1990). "Grammatical Relations," in *Meanings and Prototypes: Studies in Linguistic Categorization*, edited by S. Tsohatzidis, 587–684, London: Routledge.

Lawson, E. Thomas (1993). "Cognitive Categories, Cultural Forms and Ritual Structures," in P. Boyer, *Cognitive Aspects of Religious Symbolism*, 188–206, Cambridge: Cambridge University Press.

Lawson, E. Thomas and Robert N. McCauley (1990). *Rethinking Religion: Connecting Cognition and Culture*, Cambridge: Cambridge University Press.

Lawson, E. Thomas and Robert N. McCauley (1993). "Crisis of Conscience, Riddle of Identity: Making Space of a Cognitive Approach to Religious Phenomena," *Journal of the American Academy of Religion* 61: 201–23.

Lester, Robert (1987). *Buddhism: The Path to Nirvana*, San Francisco: Harper&Row.

Mandler, Jean (1992). "How to build a Baby: II. Conceptual Primitives," *Psychological Review* 4: 587–604.

McCauley, Robert N. and E. Thomas Lawson (1993). "Connecting the Cognitive and the Cultural," in *Natural and Artificial Minds*, edited by Robert G. Burton, 121–45, Albany: SUNY Press.

Sperber, Dan (1975). *Rethinking Symbolism*, Cambridge: Cambridge University Press.

PART IV

Beyond Theory

INTRODUCTION TO CHAPTER 13

This is the story of my introduction to scientific work, especially its experimental aspects. It is a story that, once begun, has never ceased. I invite you to accompany me on this journey. In this description of that journey, I discuss the relationship between the humanities and the sciences and how I changed my focus as a student of the world of knowledge from issues central to a humanistic program in religious studies to a slowly developing research program in search of scientific explanations.

13

Experimental Adventures

Scientific theories and the experiments that either confirm or disconfirm them are fundamental to that intellectual endeavor. My doctoral work in the humanities was replete with theories but devoid of experiment, although that is changing in interesting and significant ways. (See the publications of Joseph Carroll, who has applied the concept of evolution to Literary Materials.) I would like to describe my slow introduction to the world of science and especially into experimental work. I graduated with a PhD in the philosophy of religion in 1963, but I had already accepted a position in the Department of Philosophy and Religion at Western Michigan University in 1961 and began to teach courses in comparative religion while writing my doctoral dissertation. I also developed an interest in psychology because of discussions with behavioral psychologists as well as linguists who challenged me to *explain* religious thought and behavior rather than simply describe these phenomena. This led to a great deal of reading, (see above) especially the work of B. F. Skinner but also the works of Noam Chomsky.

In 1976 I was invited to deliver a lecture at the University of Notre Dame and there I had the opportunity to meet a very distinguished philosopher of science, Ernan McMullin. We had a good conversation about the scientific study of language. He was suspicious of the scientific character of the generative-transformational project and I was impressed by it so we had a lively discussion of the issues. Later that year I found out that the *Council for Philosophical Studies* would be holding an eight-week summer workshop on *Biology, Philosophy and the Social Sciences* to be led by Marjorie Grene and Alan Donagan and taught by a lineup of very distinguished scientists and philosophers. I decided to apply but not expecting to be admitted. I needed the recommendation of a well-known philosopher of science outside of my own institution. In desperation, I called up Professor McMullin with whom I had had only one conversation, even if it was a long one, and asked him whether he would be willing to recommend me for the workshop. Much to my surprise and excitement, he said he would be most happy to do so on the basis of the conversation we had had earlier that year. The workshop was to be held in Colorado Springs at The Colorado College and all expenses would be paid. I was ecstatic and terrified when I was notified that I was accepted. I felt woefully unprepared because the students selected all had PhD's in philosophy of science, biology, or anthropology and sociology, whereas I had a degree in the philosophy of religion. Lecturers were Stephen Gould, Richard Levins, Anthony Kenny, William Wimsatt, and four or five others. I soon became friends with Alex Rosenberg, Joanne Straumanis, and Ann Donchin all trained in the philosophy of science. We had lectures morning, afternoon, and often at night. In between we had to read many books. I had never been so academically busy in my life but loved every moment of it.

One day very soon after the seminar began Richard Levins announced that he would accept five assistants to help him with the study of harvester ant behavior in the Garden of the Gods. Each applicant for the position would have to undergo an interview. There were about twenty of us in the workshop and all decided to apply. I was last in line. When I sat before him in a nice comfortable chair, he asked me what I had studied. I told him, the philosophy of religion. Have you studied biology? He asked. No. He looked at me for a moment and then said: you are in! I was astonished. I later asked him why he had accepted me and he said: "Tom, your mind was devoid of all the many wrong ideas that people who study biology often acquire. I did not have to worry about anything interfering with what I wanted you to accomplish." Professor Levins was an amazing teacher. For example, after he had spread some food (tuna fish) around the harvester ant hole, he told each of us to choose an ant and observe its behavior. This is very difficult when you have hundreds of ants running around in all directions. But if you kept your wits about you, you chose your ant, observed its behavior, and you finally noticed that an ant would pick up some food, walk around, drop it and pick up another piece, drop it, walk around, and so on. So, what did you learn? That ants had a very small attention span and picked up and dropped food frequently. Then Levins spread some more food around and told us this time not to observe the ants but to observe the food. What astonished us was that the food slowly progressed from the edges of the clearing around the hole right down the hole. In a very little time, all the food had been successfully collected and delivered. "O. K." he said. "Now you have learned that you can have an efficient system with inefficient components." Then he spread a mixture of real food and fake food (sugar pellets and nonpareils). All of it went down the hole. Then the fake food started coming right back up out of the hole. So, the ants were able to discriminate between fake food and real food or at least the efficient system with inefficient components could. On another day we learned how to find out the ant population in the area, the different kinds of ants, by drawing a grid and placing food on various nodes on the grid and counting the variety of ants on each node of the grid. We also learned that harvester ants were very responsive both to moisture and to temperature. He illustrated this by kneeling over the hole and shouting, "Harvester Ants come out" and there was a veritable pouring of ants from the hole. Why? Not because they heard his voice but because they responded to the moisture in his breath and thought that the conditions were right for gathering food. We also learned the effect of radical differences in temperature faced by a harvester ant. When we measured the temperature on the ground it was, for example, 108F., but resting the bulb of the thermometer on a toothpick and the temperature might be 101F. Quite a difference. If there were clouds in the sky the ants were not in danger of being cooked to death, but if they had ventured outside the nest while there were clouds in the sky and then the sun appeared they were in great danger. All the ant had to do, however, was climb a short distance up a stalk of grass and it was safe. Day after day we learned many things about the behavior of ants by performing very simple experiments. I was in my element. I was learning how to be an experimental scientist. I should also mention that my wonderful student Robert N. McCauley, Bob, by this time had been admitted to the University of Chicago, and after receiving an MA in comparative religion, he switched to the philosophy department with the goal of studying the philosophy of science and his mentor was the very William Wimsatt whom I had met at this workshop. Bill and I became very good friends and have kept in touch with each other ever since.

After my summer in Colorado Springs, I came back to Kalamazoo as a new person. I was inspired to develop a genuinely interesting scientific study of religion that was theoretically sophisticated and that could, in the long run, be experimentally driven. So, I took a renewed interest in linguistics but saw now that the study of language was, in fact, a psychological study with connections to biology.

Sometime in the early 1980s, I knew enough about linguistics and specifically the complex ways in which linguists represented the structure of sentences to wonder whether it was possible to represent the structure or religious acts and specifically ritual acts in a similar way. One day, while doodling I realized that an action of any kind was very similar to a sentence. First, I went to the philosophers to see whether anyone had done interesting work on the structure of action. I could not find anything that clicked. So, I began to conjecture about how we could represent actions. I saw that every ritual consists of an agent and action and an object upon which the action is performed, for example, a priest (the agent) baptizes (the action) the baby (the object of the action). I even drew some tree diagrams to show the structure. I was quite excited and called up Bob McCauley and asked whether Ruth and I could come down to visit him and his wife Drindee in Indiana. When we got there, at a certain point I pulled out the sheets of paper on which I had written my ideas and showed them to him. I asked him whether he thought there was anything to them. Bob is a very straightforward, honest, no holds barred philosopher of science. He looked through it and after a few moments of reflection said, "No." Well, that's the way the ball bounces I thought. "Do you have any Scotch?," I asked. Why sure. So, we had a good shot of scotch and talked about many things. At a certain point in the evening, though, Bob asked me to show the stuff I had written down again and after looking it over again, said, "I think there might be something to this after all." From despair to excitement. We decided then that we would each develop these ideas further and maybe even write a paper together, which we proceeded to do in short order. Bob has a first-class mind and has the ability to handle abstractions with aplomb. In very little time he had developed the ideas I had come up with in very interesting ways. From then on, we exchanged versions back and forth and finally decided that they were worth submitting to an appropriate journal. First, I submitted the paper to the *Journal of the American Academy of Religion*. It did not take long for me to receive word that our paper had one recommendation to publish and one not to publish. So, the paper was rejected. Next, I sent it to *Religion*, edited by Ivan Strenski, and it was rejected. Then I sent it to *Current Anthropology*, edited at the time by Cyril Belshaw. He wrote and asked me for the names of twenty anthropologists who might review the paper. I did not know twenty anthropologists so I just picked names almost at random from the United States, the United Kingdom, and Europe. After quite a long wait, Belshaw informed me that while the paper had fifteen positive evaluations, it also had five negative judgments, so he rejected the paper.

After returning from Australia in 1985, where I had read a version of this paper, I told Bob that we ought to forget trying to get the paper published. Instead, we should write a book. That we did and by the end of 1985 we were well on our way to writing *Rethinking Religion: Connecting Cognition and Culture.* That book made many predictions and appealed to empirical examples. The predictions, however, lacked experimental confirmation and that bothered me. If this work was to be scientific, it required an experimental dimension.

In the late 1990s, Justin Barrett suggested to me that it was possible to test some of the hypotheses generated by the theoretical work in *Rethinking Religion* and was willing to work with me to design an experiment focused on ritual intuitions. Justin happened to have a position at Calvin College in Grand Rapids, Michigan, which is just a short drive from Kalamazoo. So, Justin made frequent trips down to Kalamazoo and we brainstormed about possible experimental designs. I was the expert on content, Justin on method, and the result was a stimulating collaboration. I have already described the experiment in the chapter on Imagining the Gods, so I will not repeat it here, but I was greatly encouraged when the experiment was so successful. The paper "Ritual Intuitions" was peer reviewed and published in the *Journal of Cognition and Culture.*

In the autumn of 2003, I made an important decision when Harvey Whitehouse asked me to help him establish the Institute of Cognition and Culture at Queen's University Belfast. Because the cognitive science of religion was developing rapidly and the more general topic of the relationship between cognition and culture was attracting considerable attention by scholars such as Dan Sperber, Larry Hirschfeld, Scott Atran, and Pascal Boyer, I jumped at the opportunity to participate in this conversation by making an academic move from Western Michigan University in Kalamazoo to Queen's University Belfast in 2004. One of my doctoral students was Joel Mort, who was just completing the writing of his doctoral dissertation so I encouraged him to join me in Belfast in this exciting new venture. We were both named International Fellows of the newly formed institute and I presented an inaugural lecture entitled, "Why the Zebra Has Stripes." Joel completed his doctoral dissertation and the next year accepted a job related to the European Office of Aerospace Research and Development. He and I successfully solicited unprecedented DoD funding for a grant to engage in scientific studies in South Africa and particularly KwaZulu-Natal. Michal Fux was one of our doctoral students and, once she had graduated with her doctoral degree, she joined our team. We were ready to engage in cross-cultural studies and the similarities between South Africa and the UK intrigued us so we embarked on a study of the contrasts between conventional knowledge and scientific knowledge, especially with regard to contagion and contamination, predation and assault, depletion of resources, and change in social status, all important themes in precautionary psychology. We designed a study to be applied both in Northern Ireland (UK) and South Africa. Participants in the study were asked to use a seven-point Likert scale: 1 = strongly disagree and 7 = strongly agree to determine their anxiety about different potential threats to their well-being. We assumed an important difference between actual and potential threats. Responses to actual threats are well understood from an evolutionary perspective: flee, freeze, or fight, whereas response to potential threats requires a precautionary account. A dangerous, hungry animal might lurk around the corner if I go in that direction (anxiety about predation or assault), what happens if I lose my position in our group (change in social status), what if I get sick from eating that new fruit (contagion or contamination), and what if our crop fails to develop (depletion of resources). We were particularly interested in differences both within a population and between populations.

Participants were presented with twenty statements, five for each domain, for example, "I worry about keeping my hands and body clean" or "I worry about not earning enough money." (Items were judged by panels of evaluators in the UK and South Africa.) We empirically verified that females, cross-culturally, are worried more about predation/assault than males and discovered that South Africans were more worried about predation/assault than their counterparts in the UK. Furthermore, non-white South Africans were more worried in all domains when compared with white South Africans. There were other findings (see Mort, Fux, and Lawson 2015), but we still have mounds of data to analyze so stay tuned. There is still work to do.

References

Mort, J., M. Fux, and E. T. Lawson (2015). "Rethinking Conventional Wisdom: Ecological Effects on Potential Danger Preoccupation Salience," *Human Ecology* 43(4): 589–99.

Conclusion

One goal of this book was to show you how cognitive science works especially when applied to the subject of religion by offering you a collection of essays that try to unpack some of religion's features. I also wanted you to know some of the personal and historical facts about my journey to the land of science and to meet some of my friends and the role that they played in that trek. CSR has now become a new discipline with exciting work published in books and scholarly journals and taught at many universities. In some instances, it has become institutionalized in various centers. Various journals pay particular attention to theoretical and experimental work in CSR, and publishers are eager to publish work in the field. When undergraduate students are exposed to CSR, many begin to identify themselves as cognitive scientists of religion and many of them go on to engaging in doctoral work in the field. Finally, one of the marks of a discipline is the publication of textbooks. One such has recently been published, authored by Claire White, and more are in the works. The International Association for the Evolutionary and Cognitive Science of Religion is now the official organization for CSR, and it has regular meetings in various international centers. CSR is here to stay.

Index

acquisition of
  cultural knowledge   36
  language   23
  religion   25
action representation system   37, 43,
    47, 48, 51, 62, 63, 117, 153
afterlife   128, 134
agency   87, 88, 90, 91, 93, 94
agency detection   108, 133, 136–8
alternative geometries   16
Antonnen, Veiko   18
artificial minds   39, 151
Atran, S.   9, 162
attention-grabbing   25, 90, 135, 149
attractor   27, 55
attribution theorists   107

balanced and unbalanced
    religions   33, 119, 120
Barrett, J.   l, 8–10, 15, 17, 33, 45, 102,
    106, 109, 111, 137, 139, 140
Bering, J.   134
Black Action Movement (BAM)   2
blank slates   13, 56
Boyer, P.   6, 8, 9, 10, 11, 17, 18, 33,
    41, 42, 90, 92, 104–7
by-product theorizing   26, 115, 120,
    134–40

chanting   116
Chomsky, N.   14, 15, 19, 24, 64, 84,
    137, 158
CI Agent   117–18
classical *vs.* connectionist debate   92
cognitive approach to religious
    materials   8, 155
cognitive representation of action
    systems   41

cognitive revolution   11, 12, 41, 55,
    132
cognitive science of religion
    first use of term   5
competence theorizing   36–8, 47, 50,
    151
conceptual relativism   72, 75
conceptual scheme   37, 75, 77, 88,
    89, 102, 116–18, 153
connectionism   52, 92
conspecific recognition   99
conspiracy theorists   107
constraints on the imagination   61
cost and benefit analysis   115, 119,
    136
costly signaling   115, 119
counterintuitive ideas, transmission
    advantage of   79
counterintuitiveness of scientific
    knowledge   65
Credibility enhancing displays
    (CREDS)   115
cross-cultural generalizations   12
cross-disciplinary co-operation   18
cultural tourism   38
culture
    evoked   6, 55, 56
    notion of   55
    transmitted   56

dispositions   26, 56, 129
doctrinal and imagistic religions   116,
    120

Eliade, M.   2
evoked culture   6, 55, 56
evolution   7, 26, 27, 33, 60, 67, 68, 91,
    115, 129, 133–5

experimental design 162
Eye-direction detector (EDD) 99

false belief recognition 100
false positives 138
"FORCE" 95

general cognitive mechanisms 87
goal demotion 118
group selection 134, 135
Guthrie, S. 6, 8, 9, 93, 102–4

hidden causes 108
Horton, R. 73, 74
Hyperactive Agency Detection Device
(HADD) 137

idealization 39
imaginary rituals 50
imagistic religion 116
innateness 92, 101, 102
Institute of Cognition and Culture 9, 162
integrating theories 27
intellectualist movement 42, 70–2
intentionality 96–7
interpretive stance 132

Jarvie, I.C. 80
journal of cognition and culture 162
judgments of ritual form 39–48

King, Martin Luther 2

launching effect 95
Leslie, A. 94
Levi-Strauss 81–4
linguistic methods applied to cultural
materials 4, 5
linguistic variability 4–6

McCauley, R. N. 3–8, 10, 24, 27, 36,
40, 41, 71, 88, 92, 108, 111, 127,
137, 138, 140, 147, 162, 163
Magic Bullet 23–4
Malinowski, B. 71, 81
Malley, B. 18, 20
Martin L. H. 3, 6, 115
mathematics as the language of
science 66

meaning 12, 15, 42, 46, 59, 76, 82,
89, 162
mechanical properties 97
modularity 92
Mort, J. 9, 20, 27, 162, 163
myths as false explanations and
symbolic descriptions 67

naturally generated narrative 93
natural selection 7, 55, 56, 62, 66–8,
87, 91, 98, 135
nature and nurture, their relation 67
Norenzayan, A. 9

object agency filter 45, 53
on-line mode of reasoning 108

participant observation 139
path of least resistance 68
Pinker, S. 12
prayer 25, 104
predictions 43, 48, 50, 51, 87, 89,
110, 111, 140, 152, 153, 159, 162
predisposition to recognize
agents 92
Principle of Superhuman
Immediacy 108
progressive and degenerating
paradigm 131
prototype ritual 109
Pyysiainen, I. 6, 8, 9, 91

rational dualism 78
reductionism 31–2, 132
reduction of behavioral psychology to
cognitive psychology 132
religious ritual competence 25, 27,
39, 50, 77
retrodiction 127, 128
ritual
action 4, 6, 16, 18, 19, 25, 26, 36,
41–3, 148–53
action representation 43–8
form 14, 152
frequency 67
proximity 49
speech 25
structures 6, 8, 41, 50, 109
Rochat, P. 26, 28

INDEX

self-propelledness 93
sense of adventure 14
sensory pageantry 118
Shared attention mechanism
  (SAM) 99
situational logic 68
Skorupski, J. 71
Slone, J. 8, 14, 27, 28, 139
slow and fast thinking 92
Sosis, R. 134
Sperber, D. 8, 16, 25, 27, 41, 55, 56,
  84, 91, 92, 135, 136, 147
Staal, F. 4, 5, 8
status change 162, 163
structuralism 3, 7, 81–3
superhuman immediacy, the principle
  of 48, 49, 108, 153
surprise, looking experiments 93
symbolist movement 71
system for the representation of
  religious ritual action 48

theological correctness 115
theoretical rituals 50
Theory of mind (TOM) 26, 98, 100

thick description 24
thought experiment 78, 128
transmission, cultural 33, 67, 89, 92,
  105, 106, 115, 128
transmitted culture 67
Trigg, R. 77
truth content 46

unconscious knowledge 50
underdetermination 37
universal principles 47–52

variability
  cultural 12, 13, 152
  linguistic 12, 13
  obstacle to generalization 12
  religious 15, 31, 49
  social life 43

well-formedness of rituals 37, 38, 41,
  44, 88, 102, 111
Whitehouse, H. 9, 30, 32, 33, 162
Wiebe, D. 3, 6, 115
Wilson, D. S. 134
Winch, P. 7

Milton Keynes UK
Ingram Content Group UK Ltd.
UKHW021829231123
433157UK00004B/194